Jallad

WITHDRAWN

Jallad

Death Squads and State Terror in South Asia

Tasneem Khalil

PlutoPress
www.plutobooks.com

First published 2016 by Pluto Press
345 Archway Road, London N6 5AA

www.plutobooks.com

Copyright © Tasneem Khalil 2016

The right of Tasneem Khalil to be identified as the author of this work has been
asserted by him in accordance with the Copyright, Designs and Patents Act 1988.

British Library Cataloguing in Publication Data
A catalogue record for this book is available from the British Library

ISBN   978 0 7453 3571 1   Hardback
ISBN   978 0 7453 3570 4   Paperback
ISBN   978 1 7837 1693 7   PDF eBook
ISBN   978 1 7837 1695 1   Kindle eBook
ISBN   978 1 7837 1694 4   EPUB eBook

This book is printed on paper suitable for recycling and made from fully
managed and sustained forest sources. Logging, pulping and manufacturing
processes are expected to conform to the environmental standards of the
country of origin.

Typeset by Stanford DTP Services, Northampton, England
Text design by Melanie Patrick

Simultaneously printed in the European Union and United States of America

To Sharmin Afsana Shuchi – brightest of the lights
in darkest of the nights

CONTENTS

ACKNOWLEDGEMENTS

Writing this book was a brutal exercise for me, especially the part where I had to sift through countless accounts of torture, executions and massacres. Two people, who not only helped me maintain my sanity but also made me smile (sing and dance, even) during this long and often tormenting process, were my children: my son Tiyash Tasneem and my daughter Tanish Tasneem. Tiyash also read an early (and, milder) version of the introductory chapter and gave excellent feedback. To them, I say 'Thank you!'

I have dedicated this book to the woman in my life (and, my partner in crime): Sharmin Afsana Shuchi. She remains the most critical reader of my writings. To her, I remain indebted – especially for her critical and challenging feedback on all the chapters.

I would like to especially thank Liz Fekete (Institute of Race Relations) for sending David Castle of Pluto Press my way. If she had not referred David to me and if David had not asked me for a book proposal, I would not have even thought of writing a book. David is an editor with superhuman patience who granted me extension after extension as I repeatedly failed to deliver the manuscript on time. There is no language in which I can properly thank him for suffering as my editor.

I would like to thank Firoze Manji, Lalon Sander, Dan Morrison and Mahfuz Sadique for their critical feedback on different parts of this book. Two other individuals in India (who shall remain unnamed, for security reasons) offered me invaluable help with my research on Maoist insurgencies across South Asia. I hope they and their comrades remain safe, especially from agents of the state.

My investigation into South Asian death squads first started with a story I published about the Rapid Action Battalion (RAB) in Bangladesh in 2006. I would like to thank Zafar Sobhan, my editor for that story on RAB, for his guidance in those early days. I would also like to thank my friends and colleagues at Human Rights Watch – Meenakshi Ganguly, Henrik Alffram, Fred C. Abrahams, Nicholas George, Brad Adams, Sam Zarifi and Ali Dayan Hasan – with whom I collaborated as a consultant researcher, investigating torture and extrajudicial executions in Bangladesh.

In different chapters of this book, some descriptions of human rights abuses and participation of human rights abusers in United Nations peacekeeping missions, are partly based on research I conducted earlier (in 2009) for the Dag Hammarskjöld Foundation (DHF). I would like to thank Henning Melber (currently Director Emeritus of the DHF) for his patronage, support and guidance as my supervisor at DHF. I would also like to thank Syeda Lubna Mehrin for her invaluable support as my research assistant at DHF. I remain indebted to Adilur Rahman Khan (Odhikar, Bangladesh), Ahmed Ziauddin (Odhikar, Bangladesh/Belgium), Angelika Pathak (Amnesty International), Shabnam Hashmi (ANHAD, India) and Mandira Sharma (Advocacy Forum, Nepal) for their contribution and collaboration.

Finally, I would like to thank Nazneen Khalil, Lubaba Nusrat Khalil, Birgitta Sandberg, Arun Ignatius and Jason Morris for offering me their counsel and company as I was writing this book. Writing is one of the loneliest exercises known to men (and women, of course). My family and friends tried their best to make sure that I would not suffer this loneliness too much.

1

INTRODUCTION:
AFTER THE COLONY

jallad noun (Hindi, Urdu, Bengali): executioner, hangman

There were the military quarters, the cantonment, and then the civilian quarters. Amritsar in 1919 was a city with a population of 160,000 – home to the Golden Temple, the holiest site of Sikhism. The old walled city with its dark and narrow streets where the natives lived in their dingy houses, stood in strong contrast with the spacious British cantonment located just outside the walls with its wide boulevards lined with trees. Residents of this part of the city were the colonial masters of Punjab, India. The colonial city was a city cut in two.[1]

Few more than 300 officers and soldiers of the British Indian Army were stationed in Amritsar at that time. They were the administrators of the British Raj, specialists on colonial domination, control and repression. And in 1919 they were dealing with a crisis of disobedience across Punjab since Mohandas Gandhi announced his first call for *satyagraha* opposing the draconian Rowlatt Act – 'a black law', as he described it.[2]

The Imperial Legislative Council in London passed the act in March 1919. It was designed to empower the Raj in imposing a permanent state of emergency in the colony, to deal with public unrest or rebellion. Emergency provisions granted by the act were: preventive detention of suspects without trial for up to two years; arrest and search without a warrant; in camera, juryless trials with an unusually low burden of proof; and stricter control and censorship of the press.[3] '[The act is] so restrictive of human liberty that [it] must be resisted to the utmost,' wrote Gandhi.[4]

And the Indians tried resisting. This movement of resistance against the Raj was at its fiercest in Punjab. Accordingly, the Raj assigned one of its top commanders to deal with the trouble. Brigadier General Reginald Dyer arrived in Amritsar and took command of the British garrison, which by then was reinforced with additional troops. More than 1,000 soldiers of the British Indian Army were now guarding the city gates.

And within these gates, a massacre took place on 13 April 1919. That day, in the afternoon, a group of protesters were holding a public meeting against the Rowlatt Act inside Jallianwala Bagh, a walled garden near the Golden Temple. Also present in the garden were pilgrims who had come to Amritsar to celebrate *Baisakhi* (the Sikh New Year) and children from nearby houses. When General Dyer was informed about the meeting, he took it as a serious act of disobedience by the Indians – an act of disobedience and rebellion against a military proclamation which he had issued earlier, banning all public gatherings in the city. In order to retaliate, he organised a special force of 90 soldiers – 50 riflemen and 40 Gurkhas (mercenary soldiers from Nepal) armed with *khukuris* (Nepalese daggers). The soldiers marched towards Jallianwala Bagh, led by their general.

When Dyer and his troops entered Jallianwala Bagh, they saw a sea of people listening to Pandit Durga Das, editor of the newspaper *Waqt*, speaking against the Rowlatt Act. What happened next was described by Nigel Collett, Dyer's biographer:

Without any warning to the crowd, Dyer gave the order to fire. The order was repeated by Captain Crampton, whistles rang out and immediately the troops opened fire. Havoc ensued. [...] The firing continued for between ten and fifteen minutes. The noise in the Bagh was a cacophony of rifle crack, bullets thumping into flesh and walls, ricochets screeching off the brickwork, the screams of 25,000 people in terror and the cries of the wounded. [...] The sight was one of horror. The vast crowd staggered aimlessly; the air filled with dust and blood; flesh flew

everywhere; men and children fell with limbs broken, eyes shot
out, internal organs exposed.[5]

Hundreds died, thousands were injured – many of them crippled
for life. We will never know the exact numbers. The Jallianwala
Bagh massacre was one of the bleakest chapters in the history of
British colonialism in India and Reginald Dyer was its author.[6] It
was also one of the earliest precedents of cold-blooded execution
without trial in South Asia, carried out in broad daylight by a
military unit. And for this sheer act of military brutality, the
general was celebrated as a hero by some of his countrymen. 'The
saviour of Punjab,' they called him when the news of the massacre
made headlines in London and became the subject of a parliamentary debate at the House of Commons.[7] When he died in 1927, a
conservative British newspaper published an obituary titled 'The
man who saved India.'[8]

In 1983, another group of saviours started roaming the streets
of Punjab. This time they were not British but Indian military and
police officers, deployed by the central government in a series of
counter-insurgency operations against secessionist Sikh militants.
During these operations, which ended in 1993, at least three black
laws were in force.[9] The National Security Act of 1980/1984 granted
preventive detention of suspects without charge or trial for up to
one year. The Punjab Disturbed Areas Act of 1983 imposed a de
facto state of emergency and empowered the security forces to shoot
to kill. They were also granted blanket immunity from prosecution
for abuses. The Armed Forces (Punjab and Chandigarh) Special
Powers Act of 1983 granted commissioned and non-commissioned
army officers the power to use deadly and disproportionate force
against civilians. It also granted them blanket immunity.

What happened during the decade-long counter-insurgency
operation was described by Patricia Gossman of Human Rights
Watch:

[The] insurgency in the north Indian state of Punjab and the brutal
police crackdown that finally ended it cost more than 10,000 lives.

Most of those killed were summarily executed in police custody in staged 'encounters.' These killings became so common, in fact, that the term 'encounter killing' became synonymous with extrajudicial execution. Many civilians were also murdered in militant attacks. Hundreds of Sikh men also disappeared at the hands of the police, and countless more men and women were tortured. [...] [The] counter-insurgency operation that ultimately crushed most of the militant groups by mid-1993, represented the most extreme example of a policy in which the end appeared to justify any and all means, including torture and murder. It was a policy that had been long advocated by senior police officials, in particular Director General of Police KPS Gill, who has had overall authority for counter-insurgency operations.[10]

The anthropologist Joyce Pettigrew wrote about the use of death squads in these operations:

Special police operations were a part of overall counter-insurgency policy. Extralegal groups operating on behalf of the state engaged in the abduction of the following categories of person: political activists; persons suspected of having association with them; lawyers who defend families whose human rights have been violated; journalists who write about such violations; and human rights workers who record their complaints. [...] The initial act of abduction sets in train a process of illegal custody and torture which often culminates in an extrajudicial execution. [...] Persons can be picked up and detained in a range of situations: by men in unmarked cars or jeeps, but also in raids, in CRPF [Central Reserve Police Force] or commando operations, in police-army combing operations, or as a consequence of counter-insurgency operations that have been conducted in specific areas. The identity of the abduction group varies.[11]

Kanwar Pal Singh Gill, the police chief who oversaw the nightmarish campaign of torture, execution and disappearance in Punjab, was celebrated as the 'super cop' and awarded the *Padmashree* (India's fourth highest civilian award) in 1989.[12] Many Indians, of course, admired him – Rahul Chandan, Gill's biographer, compared him to great military leaders like Ulysses Grant, Dwight Eisenhower and Bernard Montgomery; a former minister, Vilasrao Deshmukh of the Indian National Congress, compared him to statesmen like Winston Churchill, Abraham Lincoln and Theodore Roosevelt; another former minister, Arun Shourie of the Bharatiya Janata Party, described him as 'the one man who saved Punjab for India'.[13]

In 1971, another group of saviours were dealing with a crisis of disobedience in East Pakistan. These were the military rulers of Pakistan, who once served the British Raj as officers in the British Indian Army. Until the end, they remained loyal soldiers and servants of the empire. With the partition of India in 1947, they became the saviours of a new country.[14] Pakistan was a country cut in two: West Pakistan where Punjabis were the dominant political group; and East Pakistan where Bengalis were in the majority. Between these two parts was another country – India, colonial sibling and arch-rival. In the geography of new colonialism, West Pakistan was the centre and East Pakistan was the periphery.[15] And in 1971, the Bengali nationalists of East Pakistan were revolting. They wanted to break free from the rule of the West Pakistani generals.

The leader of the nationalists was Sheikh Mujibur Rahman (popularly known as Mujib). By demanding greater political, economic and cultural freedom for East Pakistanis, Mujib led his party, the Awami League, to a landslide victory in the national elections of 1970. The rulers in West Pakistan, however, were refusing to accept the results of the elections. This refusal resulted in a prolonged political stand-off between Mujib and the president of Pakistan, General Yahya Khan – a former officer of the British Indian Army and a veteran of the Second World War.[16]

As the political stand-off dragged on, East Pakistan became the site of a full-blown crisis by March 1971. On 7 March, Bengali nationalists organised a massive rally in Dhaka, the provincial capital. At this rally, Sheikh Mujibur Rahman launched a mass movement of civil disobedience. As his speech made it very clear, the Bengalis were ready to secede from Pakistan.[17] With this speech, the writ of the central government disappeared from East Pakistan. Bengali government employees walked out of their offices; schools, colleges and universities closed down *sine die*; thousands of protesters came out on the streets across the province; and eventually, small clashes between protesters and army units broke out in some places.[18]

With great attention, two outside observers were watching the events unfolding in East Pakistan – Richard Nixon and Henry Kissinger, the president of the United States and his national security adviser. Pakistan was a key US ally during the Cold War and they were discussing the possible next move by General Yahya Khan, their friend and protégé. 'Rahman has embarked on a Gandhian-type non-violent, non-cooperation campaign which makes it harder to justify repression [and] the West Pakistanis lack the military capacity to put down a full-scale revolt over a long period,' Kissinger wrote in a secret memo to Nixon on 13 March 1971.[19]

A few days later, to quell the Bengali rebellion in East Pakistan, General Yahya Khan ordered a military crackdown, code-named Operation Searchlight – a quick and brutal show of military power aimed at wiping out the Awami League from East Pakistan and teaching the Bengalis a lesson that they would remember for generations to come.[20] The president, Yahya Khan, assigned one of his top commanders to lead the operation, General Tikka Khan – another former officer of the British Indian Army and a veteran of the Second World War.

A little before midnight on 26 March, army convoys started moving out of the barracks and proceeded towards pre-planned targets in major cities in East Pakistan. What ensued was described by the International Commission of Jurists as 'a terrible orgy of killing and destruction, lasting some 48 hours.'[21] In Dhaka, at least three battalions – a mix of armoured, infantry and artillery troops – took part in the carnage.

In the first hour of the crackdown, a special commando unit raided the residence of Sheikh Mujibur Rahman and arrested him. A few hours later, he was flown out of Dhaka for imprisonment in West Pakistan. Other senior leaders of the Awami League, however, managed to flee from their homes and elude arrest.

6

As the commandos took Mujib into custody, three companies of soldiers marched into the Dhaka University campus. The university was the heart and brain of the Bengali non-cooperation movement and Pakistani generals saw it as the headquarters of Bengali traitors. One after another, three residential student halls were attacked with rocket launchers, mortars, recoilless rifles, machine guns and other heavy weapons. Hundreds of students were ruthlessly slaughtered inside the halls before the buildings were set on fire. Some troops moved into the residential quarters of the teaching staff. Their commanding officers were carrying hit lists with names of people targeted for execution. At least ten university professors were dragged out of their flats and shot dead. Their bodies were then thrown into a mass grave, along with the bodies of the students.

In other parts of the city, troops attacked Bengali policemen and members of the paramilitary East Pakistan Rifles (EPR). Though these groups offered armed resistance in different locations, especially at their barracks, they were very quickly overpowered. While some managed to escape, most of the policemen and EPR members present in their barracks that night were killed.

Two other areas of the city were also targeted: the old part of Dhaka and the slum areas. In old Dhaka, troops raided street after street and dragged out Hindus from their homes. Within just a few hours, thousands of Hindus were machine-gunned to death as their houses were set on fire. In the slum areas, troops carried out what they called 'slum clearance operations', in which whole streets and localities were set on fire and people sleeping in their ramshackle bamboo huts or by the roadside were indiscriminately killed. While the attacks on police stations and EPR barracks were carried out partly due to military necessity, Hindu neighbourhoods and slum areas were targeted mostly on political grounds – for Hindus and slum dwellers were seen as staunch supporters of the Awami League.[22]

As the initial phase of the crackdown was over in the morning of 26 March, a message from the headquarters congratulating unit commanders across Dhaka was relayed over the army field radio: 'You have saved Pakistan!' – a few hours later in West Pakistan,

Zulfikar Ali Bhutto of the Pakistan People's Party echoed the message as he declared 'Pakistan has been saved!'[23]

Saving Pakistan required the Pakistan Army to engage in a genocide that killed more than 300,000 Bengalis in nine months, between March 1971 and December 1971 – some estimates put the death toll as high as 3 million. It was one of the most brutal genocides after the Holocaust and the first genocide in the history of post-colonial South Asia.[24] During these nine months, East Pakistan became a laboratory of repression where new and innovative tools of terror were developed and then deployed against a mostly unarmed civilian population.[25]

Here then, we have three executioners-in-chief – Dyer, Gill, Khan – and their soldiers described as saviours for saving India and Pakistan. General Reginald Dyer is also known as the 'Butcher of Amritsar' while many Sikhs describe KPS Gill as the 'Butcher of Punjab'. General Tikka Khan is known both as the 'Butcher of Balochistan' and 'Butcher of Bengal' because of his success in saving Balochistan and failure to save East Pakistan, which became Bangladesh. This figure of the butcher is recurrent in the history of South Asia. The butchery here, of course, refers to wanton state terror in the form of military or police brutality. And these men are examples of specialists on violence who act as saviours of the state.

The revolutionary philosopher Frantz Fanon wrote about the place of these specialists on violence in colonial and post-colonial states:

The colonial world is a world cut in two. The dividing line, the frontiers are shown by barracks and police stations. In the colonies it is the policeman and the soldier who are the official, instituted go-betweens, the spokesmen of the settler and his rule of oppression. [...] [In the post-colonial state] where the rule is that the greatest wealth is surrounded by the greatest poverty, the army and the police constitute the pillars of the regime; an army and a police force (another rule which must not be forgotten) which are advised by foreign experts. The strength of the police force and the power of the army are proportionate to the stagnation in which the rest of the nation is sunk.[26]

As the pillars or the specialists, the soldiers and the policemen are responsible for saving the regime, the state and the ruling elite. This act of saving involves the systematic use of sheer, brutal violence against a civilian population to achieve a political goal: intimidating, controlling and dominating the population to ensure the state's monopoly on violence. In other words, the state deploys its specialists wherever and whenever its writ is challenged or threatened. This is the logic of state terror – brutal quelling of trouble, disorder, dissent and disobedience through military means.[27]

And through the enactment of black laws the logic of state terror is legitimised or authorised by the state. This legitimisation has two features: dehumanisation through the restriction of human liberty and proclamation of a state of exception. In this state of exception, disturbed areas are demarcated where agents of the state perpetrate otherwise illegal and repugnant acts like torture and extrajudicial execution with impunity. In these disturbed areas, people (political activists, their relatives, lawyers, journalists, human rights workers) are dehumanised because by troubling, opposing, dissenting or disobeying the writ of the state they forfeit their right to live or live in liberty. They become *homo sacers* (accursed men) – men and women who are no longer covered by legal, civil and political rights; men and women who cease being citizens and become bare lives; men and women who can be abducted; men and women who can be held incommunicado in secret detention facilities; men and women who can be tortured to death.[28]

Where exactly are these disturbed areas? This is a question we need to ask, in order to locate the seed of trouble, disorder, dissent and disobedience. Fanon presented a textual map outlining the geography of colonial and post-colonial repression. He described how the 'the greatest wealth' of the mother country is surrounded by 'the greatest poverty' of the colonies – an image of the prosperous core and the impoverished periphery. This impoverished periphery is most often the site of state terror, the disturbed area.

Marred by socio-economic injustices, these can be entire regions in a country or areas within the metropolis, like Punjab in 1919 or the present-day slums of Mumbai. These are the new colonies of the post-colonial mother country – Punjab or Manipur in India; Balochistan or erstwhile East Pakistan in Pakistan; the Chittagong Hill Tracts in Bangladesh or the Jaffna Peninsula in Sri Lanka. The trees of trouble, disorder, dissent and disobedience in the disturbed areas grow from the prolonged structural violence or the pervasive socio-economic injustices in these areas. And those in the disturbed areas who try fighting the structural violence or protest against socio-economic injustices are the first group of targets of state terror. These are the political opponents of the state: dissenting intellectuals/activists and armed rebels/insurgents.

Structural violence in the peripheries is also the root cause of the existence and rise of an underclass in the metropolis – the lumpen-proletariat. The lumpenproletariat, Fanon wrote, 'leave the country districts, where vital statistics are just so many insoluble problems, rush towards the towns, crowd into tin-shack settlements, and try to make their way into the ports and cities founded by colonial domination.'[29] 'The pimps, the hooligans, the unemployed and the petty criminal,' then, endanger the security of the new metropolis – Mumbai, Karachi, Dhaka or Colombo. They are the second group of targets of state terror: socio-economic troublemakers in need of weeding out by the state.

The lumpenproletariat, however, can also become the foot soldiers of oppression in the metropolis or the periphery. 'The oppressor,' Fanon wrote, 'who never loses a chance of setting the niggers against each other, will be extremely skilful in using that ignorance and incomprehension which are the weaknesses of the lumpenproletariat.'[30] In South Asia, then, we see the common thug or the petty criminal working as a hired gun for powerful politicians or businessmen. And sometimes the thug or the criminal also becomes a member of vigilante, civilian death squads like Salwa Judum in India or Jagrata Muslim Janata in Bangladesh.

The skilful oppressors or the specialists on violence are the dominant group in what we call the garrison state, a state where national security is the civil religion – a state where police and military commanders direct state terror campaigns against internal enemies.[31] The garrison state – also known as the national security state – is now the predominant form of government in post-colonial countries, not only in South Asia but across the globe.[32]

On this, Fanon wrote, 'The atmosphere of violence, after having coloured all the colonial phase, continues to dominate national life [in the post-colonial state]. [...] The Third World is not cut off from the rest.'[33] In this equation, post-colonial states inherit and adapt the repressive state machinery of colonialism as well as the mechanisms of colonial exploitation. These states transform themselves into national security states in the periphery of the world capitalist system.[34] Thus, the British Raj and its tributaries become five new national security states in South Asia: Bangladesh, India, Nepal, Pakistan and Sri Lanka.

As the anthropologist Jeffrey Sluka has argued, individual states engaged in campaigns of state terror are part of an international structure or network since state terror is a global phenomenon:

[At] the global level there is an international network or system of authoritarian (mostly Third World) states that employ terror as normal procedure, coupled with their (mostly First World) external or international sponsors and support system of governments and multinational corporations, particularly the arms/security industry. At the top of this system, leading by example, are the United States and its allies (particularly the United Kingdom and France), and the terror states they support, followed by other terror states outside their sphere of influence who are supported by other international patrons pursuing their own interests.[35]

The five national security states in South Asia, of course, are connected to this international structure or network. After the colonial era of the Raj, the technology of state terror in this region has developed and diffused under a new international political system that replaced the old colonial order. In this system, new and innovative technologies of state terror are widely and easily distributed by the sponsor states to their client states. And in this new system of state terror, specialists on violence no longer or very rarely resort to massacres in broad daylight. State terror has moved behind the closed doors of secret detention facilities across South Asia. However, the intensity of such terror has reached new heights in the new colonies. It was only after the days of the Raj, that death squads appeared in the streets of Bangladesh, India, Nepal, Pakistan and Sri Lanka.[36] They are backed by black laws. And as of this writing, they are in the streets – abducting, torturing and executing their targets, the *homo sacers* of South Asia.

* * *

In September 2013, the Upper Tribunal in the United Kingdom was dealing with the case of a Sri Lankan man in his late 30s. He had arrived in the UK in October 2010, with his wife and two children. Within a month, he applied for asylum and humanitarian protection status, citing the relevant provisions in European and international refugee law. In September 2011, Theresa May – the British Home Secretary – rejected the asylum application and decided that the man and his family must be removed from the United Kingdom and deported back to Sri Lanka. He then filed an appeal with a lower court, which ruled against him in January 2012. He filed an appeal against that ruling with the Upper Tribunal.

Susan Pitt and Peter Lane, judges of the Immigration and Asylum Chamber of the tribunal, found an 'error of law' in the ruling issued by the lower court. Thus, they decided to review the case afresh. Through a counsel, the man related his story – that he was the Officer in Charge (OIC) of a death squad in Sri Lanka:

[The man] maintains that from 2007 to 2009 he worked as a member of a special unit of the Sri Lankan police force. He worked in a team of twelve people drawn from different armed services and his team also included members of the criminal underworld. [He] would receive orders directly from the Deputy

General of Police and the Superintendent of Police using a mobile phone given to him specifically and uniquely for this purpose. The unit did not have a fixed location but would meet in places such as abandoned houses. The order would come to go to arrest a certain person who was a suspected LTTE member. [He] and his colleagues would be armed. They would arrest and tie up and blindfold the detainee and place them in the footwell of an unmarked vehicle. The detainee would then be handed over to other individuals working for the government, usually in an abandoned house, sometimes passing them over to men from another unmarked vehicle, sometimes taking the person to a police station, the handover location only being given at the last minute. [...] During 2009 the arrests were widened to include other civilians and members of the criminal underworld who were suspected of acting against the government.[37]

The judges found that the man, as part of a 'joint criminal enterprise', had been 'aiding, abetting or otherwise assisting' the Sri Lankan state's widespread and systematic crimes against humanity against its Tamil population: abduction, torture and extrajudicial execution. In refugee law, such individuals are excluded from asylum or humanitarian protection. Therefore, his appeal was rejected. He was a member of what we know as the white van death squads of Sri Lanka, which first appeared in Colombo and Trincomalee (eastern Sri Lanka) in 1995.[38]

Janak Bahadur Raut was running a health clinic in Kapilavastu, western Nepal. In April 2005, he was detained by Nepalese security forces who accused him of treating Maoist insurgents at his clinic. They took him to the Gorusinghe army barracks where he was kept blindfolded for 18 days and routinely tortured with electric shocks. 'Bound and blindfolded, they inflicted electric shocks on me to the point that I lost my senses,' Raut later told journalists.[39] It took him more than two years to recover from his injuries. He now leads an organisation that advocates for post-civil war justice and account-ability in Nepal.[40]

As the civil war in Nepal came to an end in 2006, a Nepalese army officer left the country and went to the United Kingdom. In 2007–2009, he attended the MA in International Relations programme at the University of Sussex. In 2008, the UK Home Office granted him indefinite leave to remain as a resident. He returned to Nepal in 2011, where he was promoted to the rank of colonel and made the commander of an army battalion in Kathmandu. In January 2013, British police arrested the officer in East Sussex where he had celebrated Christmas with his family, on vacation from his new job as a United Nations peacekeeper in South Sudan.[41]

The officer, Colonel Kumar Lama, was accused of torturing Janak Bahadur Raut in 2005, while he was the commander of the Gorusinghe army barracks in Kapilavastu. British authorities arrested Lama under the principle of universal jurisdiction, for participating in the torture of detainees as a member of the erstwhile Royal Nepalese Army.[42] During the decade-long Nepalese civil war, the army ran torture centres across the country where suspected Maoist insurgents were held, tortured and often executed.

In south-western Pakistan, security forces and intelligence agencies are waging a war against secessionist Baloch insurgents. This has been going on, in phases, since 1958. The enforced disappearances of Baloch politicians, students, shopkeepers and labourers are routine in this dirty war – they disappear and their mutilated bodies turn up a few days or even months later. As the journalist Declan Walsh described in *The Guardian*:

The bodies surface quietly, like corks bobbing up in the dark. They come in twos and threes, a few times a week, dumped on desolate mountains or empty city roads, bearing the scars of great cruelty. Arms and legs are snapped; faces are bruised and swollen. Flesh is sliced with knives or punctured with drills; genitals are singed with electric prods. In some cases the bodies are unrecognisable, sprinkled with lime or chewed by wild animals. All have a gunshot wound in the head.[43]

The campaign of state terror in Balochistan is led by the paramilitary Frontier Corps and the Directorate for Inter-Services Intelligence (ISI), Pakistan's notorious national security agency. Since 2005, human rights groups reported a dramatic increase in disappearances across the province and nearby areas – given the large number of cases, Balochistan soon came to be known as the world capital of enforced disappearances.

Mumbai is the most populous city in India. Once, it was also the capital of encounter killings. In 1993, the first batch of encounter specialists from the encounter squad of the police started operating in the city. These specialists were the celebrated saviours, glorified in the media for taking on the criminal underworld – at least five Bollywood films were released within a few years, based on the life of Daya Nayak, the most popular of the specialists.[44] Encounter, of course, is a euphemism for cold-blooded extrajudicial executions. From 1993 to 2005, the encounter specialists of Mumbai (erstwhile Bombay) managed to execute more than 600 suspected criminals.

In an interview with the BBC, Daya Nayak admitted that he 'killed 83 criminals in four years.' The leader of the encounter squad, Pradeep Sharma, told the BBC about his successful completion of 100 encounters. 'As a policeman my job is to clean the city of criminals which is what I am doing,' he said.[45] Despite the large number of executions (mostly in the slum areas) and claims of a 'clean city', Mumbai police could not wipe out the criminal underworld since most of the top gangsters fled the country and took refuge in Pakistan and the United Arab Emirates, from where they still control their gangs and extortion rackets.

Encounter killings have been rampant across India especially in the north-eastern states, Jammu and Kashmir, Punjab, states along the Red Corridor and major cities like Mumbai or Delhi. And in 2004, it spread to neighbouring Bangladesh, under a different name. There, the government raised the Rapid Action Battalion (RAB), a paramilitary force and a death squad notorious for its crossfire killings (another euphemism for extrajudicial executions).[46]

In South Asia, death squads come in different shapes and with different names – the Rapid Action Battalion of Bangladesh, the encounter specialists of India, army units of Nepal, the Frontier Corps of Pakistan or the men in white vans of Sri Lanka. They are the *jallad*s – the executioners – deployed by the post-colonial state in the new colonies and disturbed areas. In these areas, the barracks and the torture centres are the most important government facilities. These are the temples of the national security state, occupied by the priests of state terror – torture, extrajudicial execution and enforced disappearance are the rituals of their religion. And this book is their story.

The story is presented in the following chapters. Chapters 2–6 are about the death squads and their campaigns of state terror across South Asia: the men in black of Bangladesh (Chapter 2); the encounter specialists of India (Chapter 3); the royal army of Nepal (Chapter 4); the paramilitary forces and national security agencies of Pakistan (Chapter 5); and the white van death squads of Sri Lanka (Chapter 6). A commentary on state terror follows: state terror in post-colonial South Asia (Chapter 7); specialists on violence and the national security state (Chapter 8); and the international system of state terror (Chapter 9). Chapter 10, the concluding chapter, is a brief account of my own survival of torture at the hands of Bangladeshi specialists on violence.

2

BANGLADESH: MEN IN BLACK

In April 2006, top commanders representing the special operations forces of 25 countries were attending a week-long conference at a Marriott beach resort in Hawaii. The conference – titled PASOC 2006 – was a platform for exchanging ideas and developing 'multilateral methods and procedures in combating terrorism.'[1] It was organised by the United States Department of Defense, as part of its 'global war on terrorism'. PASOC is an annual event that never makes headlines in participating countries – only a few defence industry journals take note of the conference.[2] PASOC 2006, however, attracted some uninvited attention from Indonesian human rights groups.

This was because one of the Indonesian delegates at the conference was Major General Syaiful Rizal, the commander of Kopassus – the special operations wing of the Indonesian Army and a death squad infamous for human rights abuses in East Timor, West Papua and Aceh.[3] '[The United States] should not cozy up to Kopassus. [...] This is a devastating betrayal of Indonesian human rights advocates and their efforts to reform the military and its most notorious command,' the East Timor and Indonesia Action Network (ETAN) said in a statement.[4] A few other human rights groups echoed the message. This was just a minor hiccup during the conference, which was attended by delegates from Australia, Bangladesh, Brunei, Cambodia, China, Comoros, India, Indonesia, Japan, Malaysia, Maldives, Mongolia, Nepal, New Zealand, Papua New Guinea, Philippines, Russia, Singapore, South Korea, Sri Lanka, Timor-Leste, Thailand, the United Kingdom and Vietnam.[5]

Kopassus was not the only death squad represented at PASOC 2006. One of the delegates from Bangladesh was Brigadier General Chowdhury Fazlul Bari, a former commander of the Rapid Action Battalion (RAB), a paramilitary death squad. After serving as the deputy commander of RAB since its founding in 2004, he was now the counter-intelligence director of the Directorate General of Forces Intelligence (DGFI), the Bangladeshi military intelligence agency.

The United States was cosy with him too. Bari maintained an excellent relationship with US diplomats in Dhaka. And some of them were awed by his 'unmistakable swagger'. As one of them wrote in a diplomatic cable in 2005, 'As befits a Bangladesh Army officer who is a veteran of two [United Nations] peacekeeping operations, Bari is also articulate, confident, controlled and hospitable.'[6] That cable – leaked to WikiLeaks by Chelsea Manning – was the summary of an hour-long meeting 'in RAB's shiny [headquarters] near Dhaka airport.' A meeting during which Bari lectured two US diplomats about the necessity of carrying out extrajudicial executions.[7]

On the margins of PASOC 2006, Bari sat down with the political officer of the US embassy in Dhaka to discuss the history of RAB. 'I was there at the initial planning,' the general told the diplomat.[8] He then described how the special force was formed and who were its political sponsors. One of them was Khaleda Zia, the prime minister and the leader of the Bangladesh Nationalist Party (BNP). To underline how seriously the prime minister was involved in the process, Bari noted that she herself chose the all-black RAB uniform from six design alternatives.

RAB, indeed, is dressed to terrorise. Tip to toe, RAB personnel are clad in black: black bandanas, black wrap-around sunglasses, black uniform and black boots. They are the specialists on violence with unmistakable swagger. They are Bangladesh's men in black.[9]

Terror, of course, is not only in the attire. RAB is the most efficient device of state terror that the national security machinery of Bangladesh has ever developed. This machinery is programmed towards achieving two core goals: creating a permanent state of exception through black laws and the militarisation of law and order. In Bangladesh, the national security state survives as the system of governance by achieving these two goals. This is a system which enables the ruling elite (political leaders like Khaleda Zia) to deploy the specialists on violence (like Chowdhury Fazlul Bari) as saviours who use widespread and systematic violence to quell trouble, disorder, dissent and disobedience. As a case study in state terror, RAB illustrates how this system of national security achieves its goals and who are its targets.

The process of setting up a death squad as an integral part of the national security apparatus of Bangladesh had its roots in 2002. The country was ruled by military dictators from 1975 to 1990. With the return of parliamentary democracy in 1991, the old security apparatus gradually lost its relevance in the post-Cold War world. Post-9/11, Bangladeshi generals started demanding a greater say over matters of national security, against the backdrop of the 'global war on terrorism'. They proposed setting up a National Security Council and creating an elite special force that would allow them absolute control over politics of security.[10]

Then, in October 2002, the government of Khaleda Zia launched a massive project in state terror – Operation Clean Heart, a country-wide security crackdown which deployed more than 40,000 military personnel in response to a 'deterioration in law and order'. During the crackdown, the military set up hundreds of makeshift detention/torture centres (in public places like schools and stadiums) across the country. These centres were used for holding more than 10,000 detainees (political activists, common criminals and members of outlawed communist parties) arrested without charge or warrant. More than 50 of these detainees were tortured to death. According to the official explanation, all of them died of heart attacks. The crackdown ended in January 2003.[11]

In order to shield the commanders and foot soldiers of the crackdown, the government then used Article 46 of the constitution of Bangladesh that empowered the parliament to 'make provision for indemnifying any person [...] in respect of any act done by him in connection with [...] maintenance or restoration of order in any area in Bangladesh.' The parliament enacted the Joint Drive Indemnity Ordinance of 2003 that granted the security forces and government officials blanket immunity from prosecution or censure for 'any casualty, damage to life and property, violation of rights, physical or mental damage' during Operation Clean Heart.[12] This was a black law that neither suspended fundamental rights nor granted extraordinary powers to the security forces. Instead, the law retroactively created a state of exception by granting the security forces absolute legal immunity. Operation Clean Heart gave the BNP-led government a formula for creating a state of exception through immunity and a model for militarising law and order by deploying the military 'in aid of civil power'. It now set out to embed these as permanent features of the national security configuration.

In July 2003, the parliament enacted the Armed Police Battalions (Amendment) Act which revised the Armed Police Battalions Ordinance of 1979 (a law from the military era). The RAB was created according to Article 3 of the revised ordinance, while Article 13 indemnified its members by ensuring that 'no suit, prosecution or other legal proceedings shall be against any member of [RAB] for anything which is done or intended to be done in good faith under this ordinance.' The ordinance further shielded the RAB from civilian courts by creating special internal tribunals – similar to courts martial – which were given exclusive jurisdiction over RAB personnel. However, the tribunals were not empowered to try cases of murder and other serious crimes (except rape). These crimes were deliberately excluded from the list of offences for which RAB members would face trial. In other words, the law was designed to afford RAB personnel permanent immunity from prosecution for serious abuses.[13]

The revised Armed Police Battalions Ordinance of 1979/2003 also made possible the permanent deployment of a large number of military commanders and personnel as part of the RAB. This was (re)militarisation of law and order through an innovative legal strategy that integrated the military into an elite police force – a force designed for waging war on internal enemies, in the name of crime-busting, counter-terrorism and 'internal security'.

In 2014, more than 10,000 RAB members were deployed in 15 operational units (headquarters plus 14 battalions) across

Bangladesh – almost all of the RAB commanders and more than 40 per cent of the personnel were seconded from the military (army, navy and air force); personnel seconded from the police and other security forces made up the rest.[14] And between 2004 and 2014, they executed more than 900 people across the country.[15]

According to a statistical analysis by HRW (Human Rights Watch) and Benetech HRDAG (based on data from 2004, 2005 and 2006), most of the RAB victims were male; 71 per cent were between the ages 20–39; the youngest reported victim was 14 years old and the oldest reported victim was 65 years old; most of the executions took place in the Dhaka division.[16] The victims of RAB terror (abduction, torture and execution) fall into three distinct categories: opposition party activists, members of the criminal underworld and members of outlawed communist groups.

One of the victims, Sumon Ahmed Majumder, was 23 years old when he was arrested by the RAB on July 15, 2004. He was a leader of the youth wing of the Awami League, the main opposition party. Majumder and two of his cousins were picked up by the RAB in the industrial town of Tongi, a few kilometres away from Dhaka. Eyewitnesses later described how the three men were first blindfolded and then pushed into a van. They were taken to the RAB barracks in Uttara. There, inside a torture chamber, the three were mercilessly beaten with batons and metal bars. The torture went on for hours. Then, the detainees were taken to an open space inside the barracks, where Majumder's right calf was slit open with an electric drill while his cousins were forced to watch. He was eventually taken to a hospital in Tongi, where doctors tried treating his injuries – a deep laceration on the right leg and swelling on different parts of the body. He died a few hours later.[17]

A few weeks after the murder of Sumon Ahmed Majumder, the RAB executed Picchi Hannan in August 2004. Hannan was a notorious gangster running an extortion racket in Dhaka. He was one of the 23 most wanted criminals of the country. The RAB arrested him some time in June 2004 and interrogated him about organised crime syndicates in Bangladesh and India. During the interrogation, he started disclosing the names of his political sponsors – one of them was Lutfozzaman Babar, the state minister for home affairs in Khaleda Zia's cabinet.[18] Then, on 6 August, he was taken to an isolated location in Savar (north of Dhaka) and shot to death – point-blank. The execution was supervised by Chowdhury Fazlul Bari (then the deputy commander of the RAB).[19]

Picchi Hannan was a member of the lumpenproletariat who threatened the socio-economic stability and security of the new metropolis. He grew up in a slum near the Kawran Bazar business district of Dhaka as his family had migrated to the capital in order to make a living. This was the story of thousands of other children who migrated to major cities with their parents, fleeing from abject poverty in rural Bangladesh. While his father tried feeding the family by selling vegetables at a wholesale market, Hannan became a petty thief at a very young age. After joining an organised crime gang, he became a notorious gangster within a few years. Throughout his career in thuggery, he was protected by corrupt police officers and sponsored by different political parties who used him as a hired gun. And thuggery was a lucrative business, albeit with an expiry date.[20]

The RAB is designed to eliminate socio-economic troublemakers like Hannan – common criminals and petty thugs who come from the slums. These 'economic terrorists' – extortionists, black marketeers, smugglers and drug dealers – outlive their usefulness or become burdensome for their political sponsors. The RAB has executed hundreds of such gangsters and criminals since 2004. They become targets as the regular criminal justice system is too broken to deal with them.

A few months after the execution of Picchi Hannan, the RAB arrested Mofakkhar Chowdhury of the Purba Banglar Communist Party (communist party of East Bengal), an outlawed group of extreme left revolutionaries. He was one of the most influential leaders of *jonojuddho* (people's war) – the armed insurgency waged by *sarbahara* (proletariat) parties in the south-western and northern regions of Bangladesh. In December 2004, Chowdhury was arrested in Dhaka and then taken to Kushtia (in western Bangladesh), where he was shot dead near a paddy field.[21]

Mofakkhar Chowdhury was an enemy of the state who was engaged in a small war. A war in which the *sarbaharas* of the periphery wanted to overthrow the political and economic order imposed by the centre.[22] Guided by an extreme left ideology, they were responding to the conditions in rural areas which forced people like Picchi Hannan and his parents to migrate to big cities. As Chowdhury and his comrades believed, the state of Bangladesh only understood the language of violence. And through the use of violence, they wanted to challenge economic inequality and socio-political injustices. The state, of course, deployed its death squad to eliminate these internal enemies who threatened its monopoly on violence as part of their politics. The RAB launched its crackdown against *sarbahara* groups in 2004. Within just a few years, most of these groups were wiped out through the systematic use of extrajudicial executions.[23] These, in other words, were targeted political killings.

The murder of Sumon Ahmed Majumder was also a targeted political killing by the RAB, which was widely denounced by human rights groups and opposition parties. From 2004 to 2006, the RAB routinely abducted, tortured and executed Awami League leaders and activists. These cases have been rigorously documented by human rights groups, showing a pattern of widespread abuse. In all of these cases, the bodies of the victims bore marks of brutal torture – severe bruises on the legs, under the feet and on the back; broken cheek bones; swollen and bruised fingers; holes in fingers and toes; skin peeled off from the back, shoulders and arms.[24]

The Awami League, however, survived the onslaught against its leaders and workers. In 2008, Sheikh Hasina (Khaleda Zia's arch-rival) led the centre-left party to a landslide victory in the national elections and became the prime minister. During her time in the opposition, Hasina was one of the most vocal critics of the RAB and extrajudicial executions, also known as crossfire killings. In the new government, she became one of the staunchest patrons of the death squad.

It was under the patronage of Sheikh Hasina, that the RAB added a new tool to its repertoire of terror: enforced disappearance.[25]

The first three cases of enforced disappearance of opposition party workers were reported in 2009. The total number of disappearances had reached 170 by the end of 2014.[26] In at least 94 of these cases, eyewitnesses confirmed the RAB's participation in the abduction of leaders and activists of the BNP (now in the opposition).[27] Most of them were abducted from their homes or on the streets in night-time raids – they have disappeared forever, without any trace. For their families, having no dead bodies proved to be worse than having dead bodies with marks of torture.[28]

The systematic use of enforced disappearance along with torture and extrajudicial execution by the RAB crippled the BNP and other opposition parties including Jamaat-e-Islami (junior partner in the BNP-led coalition of centre-right parties). This eventually led to a de facto disenfranchisement of the BNP-Jamaat base. The BNP and all the major opposition parties boycotted the national elections in January 2014. This gave Sheikh Hasina and her party absolute control of the parliament.[29] In an ironic turn of events, the death squad that was created by Khaleda Zia has now become the principal tool of terror used by the Hasina regime against her party.

The RAB, of course, is not the first death squad in the history of Bangladesh. Indeed, the very birth of Bangladesh was resultant from a military crackdown, launched by the Pakistan Army in March 1971 – a crackdown which involved the creation of a death squad. In April 1971, as the first phase of the Pakistani crackdown – code-named Operation Searchlight – was over, senior leaders of the Awami League established a Bengali government-in-exile in India. With Indian training and assistance, thousands of Bengali men and women joined an armed insurgency against the Pakistan Army. Neither the Awami League nor the Bengalis were ready to accept defeat, despite the shock and brutality of Operation Searchlight (see Chapter 1). Pakistani generals found themselves fighting a full-blown war in a large territory surrounded by India, where their troops were massively outnumbered by a hostile population of 70 million.[30] It was time for a ruthless counter-insurgency operation.

It was during this counter-insurgency operation, that holding facilities known as 'rape camps' mushroomed across East

Pakistan. In these camps, Pakistani troops engaged in systematic and widespread rape of Bengali women. As one of their generals reportedly bragged, their goal was to 'change the bloodline of this bastard nation' through enforced pregnancy.[31] As the war came to an end in December 1971, thousands of Bengali women were rescued from the 'rape camps' – among them more than 70,000 were pregnant from rape.[32]

Pakistani troops also engaged in widespread and systematic torture. Thousands of Bengali detainees were held in makeshift torture centres and subjected to brutal torture – severe beatings with sticks and rods; hanging the detainee from the ceiling; electric shocks; pushing needles under the nail; uprooting nails; and ice slab treatment.[33] The intensity of torture was so severe that it very often resulted in the death of the detainee. In some cases, torture was also used as a mode of execution and detainees were deliberately tortured to death.

Pakistani generals decided to raise a special counter-insurgency unit or brigade – al Badr (the moon). The unit was supervised by West Pakistani officers and its members were pro-Pakistan Bengalis, recruited from the ranks of Islamist groups like the Jamaat-e-Islami and its student wing. They were trained to undertake 'specialised operations' – abducting, torturing and executing political opponents especially Bengali intellectuals. al Badr, indeed, was the first paramilitary death squad raised as part of a war effort in the history of post-colonial South Asia. Even then, the details about its organisational history and actual command structure remain sketchy given the lack of independent and credible research.[34]

al Badr was established as a special wing of the army some time in May 1971. The first batch of its commanders were trained at the Physical Education College in Dhaka. They received instructions in operating special weapons and gathering intelligence. One part of the training was hands-on, as described by the caretaker of the college building, 'They were training twice a day. After the training, they would kill a few people ... cut them up and dump them. And then they would shoot some in Rayerbazar and dump them too.'[35] Rayerbazar, a swamp near the Turag river, soon turned into a killing field where al Badr carried out mass executions and dumped mutilated dead bodies. As the death squad became fully operational by September 1971, hundreds of such killing fields appeared across East Pakistan. Bengalis named these killing fields *jalladkhana* (the house of the executioner).

A significant number of the victims were Bengali intellectuals and professionals. They were abducted from their homes during nightly raids by groups of armed men wearing black face masks or scarves. After the war was over in December 1971, some of their bodies were found in the killing fields. Most of them, however, disappeared forever – only their names were found in al Badr dossiers discovered by Bengali freedom fighters. According to one estimate, more than a thousand Bengali intellectuals and professionals were abducted, tortured and executed by al Badr.[36] The final round of these executions took place on 14 December – two days later, Bangladesh became an independent state with the surrender of the Pakistani troops in Dhaka.[37]

It was in newly independent Bangladesh, within just a few months of independence, that the first Bangladeshi paramilitary death squad was raised by none other than Sheikh Mujibur Rahman. As the leader of the independence movement, Mujib was the prophet of freedom and liberty for Bengalis in East Pakistan. He turned into a charlatan when he became the first prime minister of Bangladesh. When he returned to Dhaka after his release from a Pakistani prison in January 1972, very few could foresee the reign of terror which he would unleash on his own people. Bengalis expected Mujib to lead them in rebuilding their land ravaged by war. Bangladesh, instead, became the fiefdom of Mujib and his lackeys – a fiefdom guarded by a death squad.

Mujib did not like the idea of building a powerful army in Bangladesh. He did not 'want to create another monster like the one we had in Pakistan.'[38] Thus, he relegated the new Bangladesh Army to a largely ceremonial role and raised a new group of monsters. This was the Jatiyo Rakkhi Bahini (National Defence Force), a paramilitary death squad created in 1972.

The Rakkhis (defenders – members of the Jatiyo Rakkhi Bahini) were Mujib's private army – 25,000 loyal men recruited from the ranks of the Awami League.[39] They were trained by Indian intelligence and military officers.[40] Armed with modern automatic weapons and tasked with eliminating political opponents as well as socio-economic troublemakers, they engaged in the abduction, torture and murder of thousands of people across Bangladesh. The Jatiyo Rakkhi Bahini Act of 1972 gave them broad police powers including arrest and search without warrant.[41] The act was amended in 1974 to grant them blanket immunity from prosecution for abuses – this came after the supreme court of Bangladesh intervened in the case of a teenage boy who was tortured to death by the Rakkhis.[42]

In addition to the Jatiyo Rakkhi Bahini Act, the Rakkhis along with other security forces were granted blanket immunity from prosecution through another piece of black law – the first national security legislation enacted by the parliament of Bangladesh. This was the Special Powers Act of 1974, which not only shielded agents of the state from the courts but also provided for the preventive (without charge) and indefinite detention of individuals without trial.[43] The act was designed to terrorise and cripple political opponents, all in the name of national security and public safety.

The Rakkhis and other security forces targeted members of two opposition groups: the JSD (Jatiyo Samajtantrik Dal, National Socialist Party) and the sarbaharas (proletariats). The JSD was founded in 1972 by a group of student leaders who were once loyal to Mujib. Now they were opposing his regime through public political programmes as well as armed attacks. The sarbaharas were a group of revolutionary Maoist insurgents led by Siraj Sikder. They were waging the first jonojuddho against the new Bangladesh state.

Mujib himself blamed these groups for killing more than 4,000 Awami League workers. In a bid to crush the JSD and the sarbaharas, he declared a state of emergency in December 1974, suspending fundamental rights and shielding himself from actions by the courts.[44]

A few days later, in January 1975, the security forces arrested Siraj Sikder in the port city of Chittagong. He was airlifted to Dhaka and taken to the official residence of the prime minister. There, Mujib proposed a truce with Sikder and the *sarbaharas*. When Sikder refused to compromise, Mujib ordered his execution. Handcuffed and blindfolded, Sikder was then taken to an isolated location on the outskirts of Dhaka and shot dead – six sten gun bullets pumped into his chest.[45] According to the official explanation, he was killed as he tried escaping from custody while being transferred to the Jatiyo Rakkhi Bahini barracks in Savar. This was one of the first high-profile cases of extrajudicial execution in Bangladesh.

The execution of Siraj Sikder was followed by the execution of Sheikh Mujibur Rahman himself in August 1975. This was carried out when a group of army officers set out to overthrow the single-party dictatorship Mujib had established. These men were once disgruntled Bengali officers in the Pakistan Army – in 1971, they defected to the Bangladeshi side and took part in the war of liberation. In a tragic turn of history, they now turned their guns on the man in whose name they waged the war against Pakistan. Mujib was murdered by a group of Bengal Lancers (an elite army unit, known for its all-black uniform) in the early morning of 15 August 1975. That morning, they raided his house and shot him dead – sten gun bullets tore a large hole on the right side of his torso. Seven members of Mujib's family were also executed in cold blood during the raid. One of them was his ten-year-old son who was dragged out of the house and shot dead.[46]

The coup of August 1975 toppled the one-party dictatorship of Mujib and brought back military dictatorship to Bangladesh. The generals were back. These were men who once served in the Pakistan Army and saw themselves as defenders of Pakistan. Now, they imposed martial law and appointed themselves as the saviours of Bangladesh.[47]

The first military dictator of Bangladesh was Major General Ziaur Rahman. In March 1971, Rahman revolted against the Pakistan Army and defected to the Bangladeshi side in reaction to Operation Searchlight, becoming one of the top commanders in the Bengali war of liberation. In November 1976, he took over as the Chief Martial Law Administrator, after a series of coups and counter-coups since the assassination of Mujib. In April 1977, he installed himself as the president of the country.[48]

As a young officer in the Pakistan Army, Ziaur Rahman served in the notorious Directorate for Military Intelligence from 1959 to 1964.[49] It was quite a useful apprenticeship for the future military dictator of Bangladesh. The agency was one of the principal organs of state terror in Pakistan, known for its 'dirty ops' and political engineering aimed towards establishing the supremacy of the military in Pakistan.[50] When he became the new ruler of Bangladesh, Rahman went back to his military intelligence roots. In 1976, he established the Directorate General of Forces Intelligence (DGFI) as the top intelligence agency in the country and modelled it after the Inter-Services Intelligence (ISI) of Pakistan.[51] And like the ISI in Pakistan, the DGFI became one of the principal organs of state terror in Bangladesh. Rahman also brought the civilian intelligence agency National Security Intelligence (NSI) under his control and used it against his opponents.

Ziaur Rahman set out to create a new class of elite in Bangladesh. These were military officers who took over all positions of power in the state and society, replacing civilian bureaucrats and politicians. This was the 'Pakistan model' which turned political leaders and activists into 'anti-state elements' or 'threats to national security'.[52] Rahman took care of them by throwing them into prison en masse. According to an estimate by Amnesty International, 10,000–15,000 political prisoners were behind bars in 1977.[53] These were mostly members of the Awami League, the JSD and other left parties like the CPB (Communist Party of Bangladesh). Many of them were taken before courts martial and prosecuted for 'offences against the state and against the army, navy and air force' – the trials were held in camera, without appeal provisions. Rahman also went after a group of military officers who opposed his politics. Some of them attempted to overthrow his regime through a series of unsuccessful coups. They were prosecuted in secret military tribunals and sentenced to execution by a firing squad.[54]

These executions, however, did not stop the coup bids. In May 1981, a group of disgruntled army officers attempted yet another coup in Chittagong. And this time they assassinated Ziaur Rahman.[55] Following the assassination of Rahman, Bangladesh saw the rule of its second military dictator. This was Lieutenant General Hussain Muhammad Ershad, who took over power and proclaimed a martial law regime in 1982. Until his overthrow in 1990 through a mass movement for democracy, Ershad used the DGFI against his political opponents – activists of the BNP (led by Khaleda Zia, General Ziaur Rahman's widow) and the Awami League (led by Sheikh Hasina, Sheikh Mujibur Rahman's daughter).[56]

It was under the command of Ershad that the Bangladesh Army intensified its counter-insurgency campaigns in the Chittagong Hill Tracts (CHT, in south-eastern Bangladesh). These campaigns were originally launched by General Ziaur Rahman in 1977. This, in effect, was Bangladesh's first dirty war against the people of its periphery – indigenous *jumma*s of the hills, who were revolting against the Bengali ethnonationalist rulers of new Bangladesh.[57] As part of the counter-insurgency offensive in this new colony, the army and paramilitary Bangladesh Rifles (BDR) perpetrated horrific abuses: massacres, torture, enforced disappearance, extra-judicial execution and the rape of *jumma* women.[58] This campaign of state terror, indeed, was modelled exactly after the campaign of state terror unleashed by the Pakistan Army against the Bengalis of East Pakistan. And to this day, even after the signing of a peace treaty between the government and *jumma* insurgents that brought an end to the armed conflict in 1997, the CHT remains the most militarised region of the country, where the Bangladesh Army and Bengali Muslim settlers perpetrate abuses with impunity.[59]

The political history of Bangladesh is also the history of the organs of terror that were developed by its rulers – al Badr (1971); the Jatiyo Rakkhi Bahini (1972); the DGFI (1976); the Rapid Action Battalion (2004). It is also the history of how the political leaders and specialists on violence of this young state have developed the machinery of state terror by revising and updating the models of terror created by their predecessors. This is a model which uses black laws to indemnify the specialists on violence and militarise law and order – a model that enables the *jallad*s of Bangladesh to roam the streets with 'unmistakable swagger'.

3

INDIA: BRUTAL ENCOUNTERS

The first bullet pierced the ribs and the left lung; the second bullet pierced the liver, diaphragm and the ribs; the third bullet pierced the intestines and vertebra; the fourth bullet pierced the stomach, pancreas, spleen, liver, diaphragm, heart, ribs and the left lung; the fifth bullet pierced the pelvic cavity, uterus, vagina and the rectum; the sixth bullet pierced the intestines; the seventh bullet pierced skin and muscle only; and the eighth bullet pierced skin and muscle only. And there were three bruises: one on the left forearm above the wrist; one on the right forearm above the wrist; and one on the right leg above the heel.[1]

The soldiers broke down the door and rushed into the house some time after midnight on 11 July 2004. They were looking for a woman named Hentoi, who was a suspected member of an insurgent group. They claimed she was a corporal of the People's Liberation Army (PLA, an insurgent group) and an expert in making improvised explosive devices. They also held her responsible for masterminding a series of bomb attacks against the Indian security forces. Hentoi did not live in this house and no one knew who she was or where she lived.

After failing to find the suspected PLA corporal, the soldiers instead detained Thangjam Manorama Devi, the daughter of the house. This 32-year-old woman did not have a criminal record. Her family, friends and neighbours later claimed that she was just a quiet and friendly person who made a humble living by weaving clothes. She also worked as a social worker, organising cultural festivals and clean-up drives in the neighbourhood.[2]

The soldiers dragged Manorama out of the house and took her to the courtyard. Her mother and two brothers were forced to stay indoors. The family could hear her screams as she was being beaten mercilessly. The soldiers also waterboarded her using a container and a towel which they took from her mother's kitchen. They were questioning her about her presumed ties with insurgent groups and the arsenal of illegal weapons she was supposedly hiding somewhere. Then, she was officially put under arrest as her captors prepared an 'arrest memo' and gave it to her family. They pushed her into a vehicle and drove away. This was the last time her family and neighbours saw her alive.

Manorama was taken away from her home in Bamon Kampu, a village near Imphal – the state capital of Manipur, in north-eastern India. Her mutilated and bullet-ridden body was dumped by the roadside some hours later. The body was found, half-naked, four kilometres away from her house. As the autopsy of the body revealed, she had been executed with eight bullets. During the autopsy, the doctors observed that her 'vaginal orifice [had] marks of injury'. However, since a bullet wound had mangled her pelvic cavity and vagina, they could not determine if she had been raped. At a later stage, forensic tests revealed signs of rape – semen on her petticoat.

A few days after the execution of Manorama, a group of elderly women gathered to protest in front of the Kangla Fort – the headquarters of the security forces in Imphal. They were enraged by the sheer brutality inflicted upon Manorama's body. The women took off their clothes and unfurled a banner that read, 'Indian army rape us' – they stood naked at the gates of the fort and asked the soldiers to come out and rape them as they had raped Manorama. As one of the protesters later said,

> Manorama's killing broke our hearts ... They mutilated her body and shot her in the vagina. We mothers were weeping ... We shed our clothes and stood before the army ... Maybe this way [the army would] spare our daughters.[3]

Within a few days after the protest, the police arrested the women and sent them to prison. They were detained under the National

Security Act of 1980 – a law ostensibly designed for dealing with people who act 'in any manner prejudicial to the defence of India … [or] security of India.'[4]

Thangjam Manorama Devi was tortured, raped and executed by the Assam Rifles – one of the oldest paramilitary forces in South Asia, also known as the 'sentinels of the north-east'.[5] More than 63,000 soldiers of the Assam Rifles are currently deployed as part of seven command wings and 46 battalions across the seven north-eastern states of India.[6] Abduction, torture and execution of internal security threats like Manorama are part of their counter-insurgency duties in the north-east.

The Assam Rifles had its roots in the Cachar Levy, a ragtag militia of 750 men raised by early British settlers in 1835, during their conquest of the Barak and Surma valleys. The levy was responsible for guarding British settlements and tea estates against 'depredations of wild hill tribes'. Within a few decades, this militia grew in size and became an integral part of the violent colonial conquest of the entire north-east. In 1917, after several name changes, it became the Assam Rifles – an efficient colonial army in charge of subjugating hundreds of 'warrior tribes' and millions of 'tribal' natives.[7]

The colonial subjugation of the north-east continued even after the end of the British Raj in 1947, as the central government of newly independent India embarked on a mission of recolonising the seven sister states of the north-east: Assam, Arunachal, Manipur, Meghalaya, Mizoram, Nagaland and Tripura. These became the new colonies where separatist movements and insurgent groups started challenging and opposing the Indian state.[8] In the geography of new colonialism, the seven sister states made up the periphery of new India – connected to the mainland through a narrow land corridor wedged between Nepal, Bangladesh and Bhutan. And this periphery had always been marred by chronic poverty. According to statistics published by the Indian Planning Commission in 2012, more than 15 million people in India's north-east lived below the poverty line.[9] It was against this post-colonial backdrop that the Assam Rifles emerged as a death squad responsible for systematic campaigns of state terror in the north-eastern periphery.[10]

In 1987, the Assam Rifles first attracted wide international attention for its abuses in post-independence India, as it launched a security crackdown in the Senapati district of Manipur. This crackdown – carried out between July 1987 and October 1987 – targeted the village of Oinam and 30 other neighbouring villages, following an insurgent attack on an Assam Rifles outpost in the area. The villages were put under a complete lockdown for months. During this lockdown, Assam Rifles soldiers engaged in horrific abuses against the villagers: hundreds of villagers were subjected to brutal torture; village churches were used as makeshift detention facilities and torture centres; many women were sexually assaulted; at least 125 houses were burnt down; grain stores, vegetable plots and livestock were looted. The crackdown was code-named Operation Bluebird.[11]

During this operation, at least 14 villagers were shot dead by the soldiers. According to the official explanation provided by the Assam Rifles, these villagers were killed in 'armed encounters' (gunfights) or 'while trying to escape' from custody. However, investigations by local and international human rights groups have established a different version – the villagers were executed in cold blood.[12] This was one of the earliest cases of encounter killings in Manipur.

In November 2000, the Assam Rifles again attracted international attention after its soldiers gunned down ten people (including a 62-year-old woman) waiting at a bus stop near the village of Malom in Manipur. The soldiers claimed that the victims were killed during an armed encounter with Manipuri insurgents who attacked their convoy. According to eyewitness accounts, however, it was a cold-blooded mass execution of unarmed and innocent civilians.[13] When the news of this brutal massacre reached Imphal, it prompted Irom Chanu Sharmila, a 28-year-old Manipuri poet, to begin the world's longest hunger strike, demanding the repeal of the black law that authorised Assam Rifles operations in Manipur.[14] The government responded to Sharmila's hunger strike by putting her in prison on a charge of attempted suicide. In November 2014, Sharmila completed the 14th year of her hunger strike.[15]

Encounter is one of the most potent tools of terror used by the Assam Rifles and other security forces throughout the north-east.

Indeed, according to the official explanation offered by the Assam Rifles, Thangjam Manorama Devi was also killed in an encounter as she was trying to escape from custody. Between 1979 and 2012, at least 1,528 extrajudicial executions were carried out by the security forces in Manipur – most of these victims were supposedly killed during 'armed encounters' or 'while trying to escape'.[16] In 2013, a judicial commission of inquiry investigated some of these cases and found evidence of premeditated executions, often preceded by torture.[17]

In India, the executioners – popularly known as encounter specialists – have been active across the country especially in the seven sister states, the northern state of Jammu and Kashmir, the north-western state of Punjab, states along the Red Corridor and major cities like Mumbai. They are the sentinels and saviours of India, deployed by the state against terrorists, extremists and gangsters. As an integral part of the security forces, these encounter specialists are the pillars of the Indian national security state. Backed by national security laws that grant them blanket immunity, they operate in disturbed areas in order to protect the Indian state from internal security threats like Thangjam Manorama Devi or the villagers of Oinam. In the peripheries of new India, like their colonial predecessors, they act as the spokesmen of the central government, speaking the language of abuse and murder.

In their campaigns of terror across the country, the security forces are backed by a plethora of black laws. These laws, by design, deprive Indian citizens of their fundamental rights and grant the security forces extraordinary powers. Among these, the Preventive Detention Act of 1950, the Unlawful Activities (Prevention) Act of 1967, the Maintenance of Internal Security Act of 1971 and the National Security Act of 1980 have been used for the preventive detention of suspected terrorists and extremists (including elderly Manipuri women); the Armed Forces (Special Powers) Act of 1958 has been used for deploying military and paramilitary units in the new colonies and disturbed areas; the Terrorist Affected Areas (Special Courts) Act of 1984, the Terrorist and Disruptive Activities (Prevention) Act of 1985 and the Prevention of Terrorism

Act of 2001 have been used to authorise India's own war against terrorism.[18]

The most draconian of these laws, the Armed Forces (Special Powers) Act of 1958, was first enacted for dealing with separatism in Nagaland – it was later extended to all the north-eastern states. Between 1983 and 1997, a version of the act was in force in the state of Punjab. Since 1990, another version of the act has been in force in the state of Jammu and Kashmir. The act enables military and paramilitary personnel to engage in counter-insurgency operations in 'disturbed areas', wherever 'the use of armed forces in aid of civil power is necessary.' In these areas, the security forces are granted enhanced powers to use lethal violence against civilians. They are also shielded from prosecution or censure for abuses. Indeed, the Assam Rifles soldiers responsible for the murder of Thangjam Manorama Devi, the siege of Oinam and the massacre of Malom were protected through a version of the law in force in Manipur.[19]

Extrajudicial executions, enforced disappearances and torture by the security forces have been most rampant in the state of Jammu and Kashmir – one of the most militarised and contentious regions of the world. With the partition of India in 1947, Kashmir became the site of 'South Asia's longest war' involving India, Pakistan and China. The territorial dispute over Kashmir has resulted in four wars: the Indo-Pakistani war of 1947–1948, the Sino-Indian war of 1962, the Indo-Pakistani war of 1965 and the Indo-Pakistani war of 1999.[20] In other words, the state has become a permanent war zone (or a 'high security zone', as Indian national security experts would describe it) since the end of the British Raj.[21]

Since 1989, Kashmir has also been the site of India's war against its internal enemies: separatist Kashmiri insurgents and ordinary Kashmiris opposed to Indian rule of their homeland. Indeed, India has always tried to govern the Kashmiris through coercion, without the consent of the governed.[22] As reported in an opinion poll published in 2010, 43 per cent of respondents in Jammu and Kashmir wanted Kashmir to become an independent state – this figure was as high as 95 per cent in the Kashmir Valley division and as low as 1 per cent in the Jammu division.[23] In the same poll, 43 per cent of respondents in Jammu and Kashmir identified human rights abuses as the main problem in their lives – this figure was as high as 88 per cent in the Kashmir Valley division and as low as 3 per cent in the Jammu division.[24] Jammu is the only region in the state where Hindus and Sikhs (predominantly Dogras and Punjabis) are in the majority. The majority of Kashmiris, on the other hand, are Muslims. Religion is an important marker of the conflict in the region – a marker which is often used by the Indian government to describe Kashmiri separatism as *jihadism* or pro-Pakistan extremism. Many Kashmiris, however, identify their separatism as a secular struggle for an *azad* (independent) Kashmir – a struggle for their right to self-determination.

In order to subjugate the Kashmiris, the central government of India has deployed more than 600,000 troops in Kashmir as part of its counter-insurgency operations. As the narrators of a PBS documentary described in 2004, 'When we arrived in Kashmir, we saw soldiers everywhere, peering from the tops of balconies and peeking out of bunkers on street corners.'[25] The soldier-to-civilian ratio in the region is staggering – the highest in the world. There is at least one Indian soldier deployed for every 17 residents of Kashmir.[26]

One of the Indian security forces deployed in Jammu and Kashmir is the Rashtriya Rifles – one of the most well-equipped counter-insurgency forces in the world and one of the most expensive. In its defence budget for 2012–2013, the government of India allocated INR2.52 billion (US$43.22 million) to sustain the Rashtriya Rifles' counter-insurgency operations[27] – a colossal sum of money for deploying more than 65,000 soldiers of the Rashtriya Rifles in 65 battalion formations across the state.[28] The force was raised in 1990, ostensibly as a paramilitary unit for curbing separatist insurgency in Kashmir. Within a few years, however, it became a de facto branch of the Indian Army due to its composition. All the soldiers and commanders of the force are deputed from the regular army. And like the Assam Rifles in the north-east, the Rashtriya Rifles is the principal organ of state terror in Jammu and Kashmir.[29]

In the words of a Kashmiri human rights group, 'The Indian state's governance of [Kashmir] requires the use of discipline and death as techniques of social control.'[30] Between 1989 and 2009, the Indian security forces were responsible for more than 70,000 deaths in Kashmir. They were also responsible for more than 15,000 enforced disappearances of Kashmiris.[31] Since 1990, Kashmiri human rights lawyers have filed thousands of *habeas corpus* (produce the body) petitions trying to locate people who went missing after being detained by the security forces. Most, if not all, of these petitions have been unsuccessful.

And sometimes, the human rights lawyers themselves have gone missing. In one such case, in March 1996, the Rashtriya Rifles abducted the lawyer Jaleel Andrabi in the city of Srinagar. Three weeks later, his mutilated and decomposed body was recovered from a river. He had been executed after gruesome torture.[32] The murder was part of a campaign aimed at terrorising human rights activists in the Kashmir valley. The campaign, however, failed to deter their tireless work in defence of Kashmiri victims of torture, enforced disappearances and encounter killings.

Ten years after the murder of Andrabi, another human rights lawyer, Parvez Imroz, first discovered the existence of secret and unmarked mass graves in Kashmir – he was investigating cases of enforced disappearance after failing to establish the whereabouts of the victims through *habeas corpus* petitions. Investigating deeper, he went on to expose a network of secret graveyards across the region.[33] Between 2006 and 2009, Imroz led a group of human rights researchers who mapped 2,700 unmarked graves in 55 villages of three districts. There were more than 2,943 bodies in these graves – 154 graves with two bodies and 23 graves with more than two bodies. As Imroz and his team expanded their search to cover more villages and districts, the total number of unmarked graves shot up to more than 6,500.[34]

These were the graves of the victims of encounter killings between 1990 and 2009, who had been buried secretly by the security forces. In the police records, these killings were invariably described as cases of armed encounter between the Indian security forces and Pakistani infiltrators. However, Imroz and his team were able to establish the identity of at least 50 victims. All of them were Kashmiri civilians – among them, at least 16 had been executed by the Rashtriya Rifles; four had been executed by the Special Operations Group (SOG) and two had been executed by the Special Task Force (STF).[35]

In 2012, Imroz and a group of human rights advocates published a report presenting the findings of a two-year-long investigation into 214 cases of human rights abuses by the security forces in Kashmir: 124 extrajudicial executions, 65 enforced disappearances, 59 cases of torture and nine rapes (some cases involved multiple abuses). The report identified 500 perpetrators in these cases: 96 personnel of the Rashtriya Rifles; 129 personnel of the regular army; 123 personnel of different paramilitary units; 111 policemen; and 31 government-sponsored militants.[36]

These cases were just a fraction of the abuses perpetrated by Indian security forces since the outbreak of a separatist insurgency in 1989. Also, since 2008, the security forces have been using lethal violence to disperse pro-independence protest rallies and demon strations. Between 2008 and 2010, at least 150 Kashmiri protesters were gunned down in broad daylight as they were taking part in largely peaceful demonstrations.[37]

Parvez Imroz's investigation exposing the mass graves of Kashmir was reminiscent of an earlier investigation by Jaswant Singh Khalra, a Sikh human rights activist who was trying to locate the victims of enforced disappearances in the city of Amritsar. This was in 1995, after the end of counter-insurgency operations against Sikh militants in the north-western state of Punjab. During the investigation, Khalra discovered official records that revealed a secret programme of mass cremations. According to Khalra's estimate, the Punjab Police burnt more than 6,000 bodies at the cremation grounds of Amritsar during the counter-insurgency operations. These were the bodies of young Sikh men executed by encounter specialists of the police and other security forces. The investigation led to Khalra's own disappearance and subsequent murder in October 1995, following his abduction by commandos of the Punjab Police.[38]

The counter-insurgency operations in Punjab that took place between 1983 and 1993 involved the systematic use of encounter killings by police and paramilitary death squads – killings that were hailed by a large number of Indians as heroic actions against treasonous Sikh militants (mostly young men) who threatened the security and integrity of the Indian republic. It was the first time the Indian state was faced with a religion-based insurgency within it borders. The counter-insurgency models that were first developed in Punjab were later used for dealing with the insurgency in Kashmir. In both cases, Indian security forces relied on brutal violence (executions) and sinister concealment (secret cremations and graves) to successfully re-establish the state's monopoly on violence in the peripheries.[39]

Despite their formidable success in the brutal quelling of separatist insurgencies in Punjab, Kashmir and the north-east, Indian security forces are now facing an insurmountable counter-insurgency challenge in the so-called Red Corridor, the site of a 'people's war' waged by the Communist Party of India (Maoist), a revolutionary group. The Maoist insurgents – also known as Naxals – control large swathes of territory in at least six Indian states along the corridor: Andhra Pradesh, Bihar, Chhattisgarh, Jharkhand, Odisha and Telangana. These are also some of the poorest regions of India – about 70 per cent of lower-caste *adivasis* (indigenous people) in these states live below the poverty line. They also endure systematic structural violence or socio-economic injustices perpetrated by the state and upper-caste landowner classes.[40]

The Naxals take their name from the village of Naxalbari in West Bengal, which was the site of the first 'people's war' launched by Indian Maoist groups in 1967. Since then, the Maoists have waged a number of such wars in different parts of the country – in each case, their insurgency has been brutally quelled by Indian security forces through the systematic use of encounter killings and widespread torture in custody. However, the most recent version of the 'people's war' is yet to be crushed by the security forces, despite their campaigns of violence and terror in the Red Corridor.[41]

This is primarily due to the current composition of the People's Liberation Guerrilla Army (PLGA), the armed wing of the Communist Party of India (Maoist). The current 'people's war', in effect, is a class-based conflict between the Indian state and some of its most downtrodden citizens – *adivasi*s and landless peasants of the periphery.[42] Since 2005, as part of the PLGA, they have been resisting the central government and its economic development plans that involve handing over *adivasi* land to multinational mining companies keen on exploiting the vast reserves of natural resources: iron ore, coal, bauxite, manganese and other valuable minerals. In other words, the PLGA is now a resistance army, as opposed to an army of ideological cadres.

To quell the armed rebellion of these Maoist *adivasis* and peasants, the central government has deployed thousands of paramilitary troops in the Red Corridor. More than 100,000 troops of the Central Reserve Police Force (CRPF), the Border Security Force (BSF) and other security forces are currently deployed in the states worst hit by the Maoist insurgency. Like the Assam Rifles, the CRPF (erstwhile Crown Representative's Police, or CRP) was a colonial paramilitary force – established in 1939 for protecting British settlers in different parts of colonial India.[43] It is currently the largest paramilitary force in India, deployed in 232 battalion formations across the country.[44]

Across the Red Corridor, as part of their counter-insurgency operations, Indian security forces perpetrate brutal abuses – torture, encounter killings and rape – against suspected Maoist insurgents and *adivasi* villagers.[45] In a campaign of systematic persecution of dissent, they also target human rights activists and academics who are advocates of *adivasi* rights as well as critics of the central government's iron rule in *adivasi* areas.[46] In recent years, environmental rights groups have also been targeted because of their opposition to large-scale mining projects in the region.[47]

One of the key features of India's war against Maoist *adivasis* and landless peasants is the deployment of civilian militias sponsored and armed by the government. In 2005, using a provision in the Police Act of 1861 (a law from the colonial era), the government started recruiting civilians as Special Police Officers (SPO) in the state of Chhattisgarh. These recruits – mostly common criminals and thugs from the upper-caste, landowner classes – were organised into a new militia force named Salwa Judum (purification hunt). Between 2005 and 2008, until the Indian supreme court declared the organisation to be illegal and unconstitutional, members of Salwa Judum perpetrated horrific abuses across Chhattisgarh: violent raids on *adivasi* villages; the forced displacement of the *adivasi*s from their villages to government-run camps; and the widespread rape, torture and murder of *adivasi* villagers. Even after the disbanding of Salwa Judum under a court order, the government has continued recruiting and deploying Special Police Officers in Andhra Pradesh, Bihar and Jharkhand. In these states, Special Police Officers have invariably engaged in campaigns of terror against *adivasi*s and landless peasants.[48]

Another notable feature of India's war against the Maoists is the use of UAVs (Unmanned Aerial Vehicles) or drones. India first deployed military drones during the Indo-Pakistani war of 1999 in Jammu and Kashmir. Then, since 2013, surveillance/reconnaissance and combat drones have been used as part of counter-insurgency operations in Andhra Pradesh, Chhattisgarh and Odisha to locate Maoist insurgent camps.[49] These drones are supplied by Israel, the world's largest exporter of drones and one of the major suppliers of weapons to India.[50]

Since 1999, India has been building its fleet of drones with Israeli Searcher and Heron systems. According to arms trade data available via the Stockholm International Peace Research Institute (SIPRI), India procured at least 176 Searcher and Heron drones worth more than US$1 billion, between 1999 and 2014.[51] Most of these drones are now being used for counter-insurgency operations in the Red Corridor – a fact that Israel proudly uses in marketing its drones to other buyers across the globe. Heron drones were first used by the Israel Defense Forces (IDF) during Operation Cast Lead in Gaza between December 2008 and January 2009. These drones were also used by the ISAF/NATO forces in Afghanistan between 2009 and 2014. Israeli Searcher drones were also used by the Sri Lanka Air Force against the separatist LTTE rebels during the final phase of the Sri Lankan civil war.[52]

The money spent by the Indian government for procuring high-tech Israeli drones to quell the Maoist insurgency is just a small share of its colossal military budget. In 2013, India had a military budget of INR2.53 trillion (US$41.9 billion) – this was 2.4 per cent of its GDP. In 2014, the budget was raised to INR2.84 trillion (US$45.2 billion). This budget is for sustaining the largest military and state security machinery in South Asia.[53] The Indian armed forces have 1,346,000 active soldiers and commanders: 1,150,900 in the army, 127,200 in the air force, 58,350 in the navy and 9,550 in the coast guard. Indian paramilitary forces are also the largest in the region, with more than 1,400,000 troops. Apart from the Assam Rifles and Rashtriya Rifles, these include: the Border Security Force (230,000 troops), the Central Reserve Police Force (229,000 troops) and State Armed Police forces (450,000 troops). These paramilitary forces are now deployed across the country as part of different counter-insurgency operations in India's peripheries.

Meanwhile, the Indian state has also been waging another internal war in its metropolises. This is led by the police and its encounter squads in major cities like Delhi and Mumbai – the capital of the country and the centre of business and commerce. These cities are home to India's ruling elite and its burgeoning middle class. Some of the most famous residents of Mumbai are Indian billionaires best known for their great wealth and opulence. On the other hand, Asia's largest slum is also in Mumbai – the Dharavi slum is home to more than a million Indians who have migrated to the city from the peripheries of India. More than 5 million people (41 per cent of the city's population) live in the slums of Mumbai – a city of opulent wealth and abject poverty. The city is also the birthplace of India's most celebrated encounter squad.

The first person ever killed by an encounter specialist in India was Manya Surve, a notorious gangster who specialised in daredevil armed robbery. Surve was born in a village near the city of Ratnagiri (in south-western India). At a very young age, he migrated to Mumbai (then named Bombay) with his mother and stepfather. Between 1969 and 1980, he emerged as the leader of a criminal gang that recruited its members from Dharavi and other slums in the city. In 1981, after carrying out a series of armed robberies in the heart of Mumbai, he became one of the most wanted men in the city. The Mumbai Police (Bombay Police) set up a special squad to track down Surve and his associates. The squad finally got hold of him on 11 January 1982 – he was shot dead by India's first encounter specialist Isaque Bagwan in the Wadala district of Mumbai. The police registered the extrajudicial execution as a death 'during encounter'.[54]

The history of encounter killings in Indian cities correlates with the geography of internal migration. Millions of Indians every year migrate from the peripheries to the metropolis. Many of them become part of the lumpenproletariat of the city. These are the people who threaten the city's economic security and stability as they engage in petty crimes and gang violence. Some of them also engage in terrorism against the state. In 1993, the Mumbai Police first set up its encounter squad (officially named the Bombay Police Detection Unit) to crackdown on an organised crime gang founded by another migrant from Ratnagiri – Dawood Ibrahim Kaskar, the dreaded leader of the Indian Mafia (also known as the D-Company). Ibrahim and his gang were responsible for a series of car bomb explosions across Mumbai on 12 March 1993. These bomb attacks – which killed more than 250 and injured more than 700 – were carried out in retaliation for the anti-Muslim riots in the city which took place in January 1993, killing more than 500 Muslims and 250 Hindus. Following the attacks, Ibrahim fled India and went into exile in the United Arab Emirates. In 2003, the United States declared him a 'global terrorist' due to his ties with al Qaeda. He is now based in Pakistan, living under the protection of the ISI (Pakistan's main intelligence agency).[55]

The history of India's independence is the history of coercive recolonisation campaigns and brutal repression in the new colonies – the seven sister states in the north-east and Jammu and Kashmir in the north. It is also a history of pervasive structural violence and massive economic exploitation endured by the people of the peripheries – the *adivasis* of the Red Corridor and internal migrants living in the slums of Mumbai, Delhi, Kolkata and other metropolises. Repression and exploitation are the two core principles of the post-colonial order in India – an order which is now being protected by India's saviours and sentinels: the encounter specialists of paramilitary and police death squads. Some of these death squads, like the Assam Rifles and the CRPF, were once integral parts of the colonial machinery of repression, designed by the administrators of the British Raj – machinery of repression that was inherited and then perfected by India's ruling elite through the enactment of black laws and the creation of new paramilitary forces like the Rashtriya Rifles. For the people of the peripheries and the new colonies, independent India indeed is nothing but a revised and updated version of colonial India, where discipline and death are still the 'techniques of social control'.

4

NEPAL: THE ROYAL ARMY

The members of the fact-finding mission reached Doramba after hiking for an hour in the early morning on 27 August 2003. Due to the foggy weather and low clouds, the village in central Nepal was inaccessible even by air – the helicopter that carried the team from Kathmandu had to make a landing near a hill two kilometres outside the village. There were five members in the team: Krishna Jung Rayamajhi, a former justice of the supreme court; Prem Bahadur Bista, a former attorney general; Kanak Mani Dixit, a journalist; Harihar Osti, a forensic pathologist and Hari Phuyal, a lawyer. They were sent to Doramba by the National Human Rights Commission (NHRC) of Nepal to investigate a massacre that had taken place ten days earlier. When they arrived in the village, the investigators found its residents 'in the grip of fear', still reeling from the shock of witnessing a mass murder that was making headlines across South Asia.[1]

The following morning, the villagers took the NHRC investigators to the site of the massacre. There, the investigators collected a few items of evidence: one *dhaka topi* (Nepali cap), one toothbrush, two pocket combs, seven slippers, 17 empty bullet shells, pieces of green cloth used for tying hands and broken pieces of human skull. Then, they were taken to a new graveyard located just a few metres from the crime scene. There were 18 fresh graves in three rows.

The villagers helped the investigators in cordoning off the area and exhuming the graves of the victims. This was the first forensic excavation – *shabotkhanan* – in Nepal. Harihar Osti, the forensic pathologist, entered the graves one by one and examined the dead bodies – there were five female bodies and 13 male bodies. He checked the wounds and scars on these bodies by measuring their length and width; Hari Phuyal, the lawyer, took detailed notes about Osti's findings; Kanak Mani Dixit, the journalist, photographed and filmed the whole process. The excavation revealed evidence of a cold-blooded mass execution – all of the victims had been shot dead from a very close range, with their hands tied behind their backs. Most of the victims had been shot in the head, which fractured their skulls – four of the victims had been shot in such a manner that the upper parts of their heads were entirely missing. After completing the forensic examination, the team reburied the bodies and returned to the village in the evening. There, a man secretly handed over a roll of film to Dixit. This roll contained photographs of the bodies, taken one day after the execution. During their stay in Doramba, the investigators also collected eyewitness testimonies from the villagers – these were recorded by Krishna Jung Rayamajhi and Prem Bahadur Bista. After spending four days in Doramba, the team returned to Kathmandu and submitted its findings to the NHRC.

Based on the technical/forensic evidence and the eyewitness statements collected by the investigators, the NHRC published a report a few days later. It was a detailed account of the Doramba massacre which was carried out by a company (80 soldiers) of the Royal Nepalese Army (RNA). The NHRC held the royal army responsible for extrajudicial executions in violation of the laws of war, especially 'Common Article 3' of the Geneva conventions (relating to the treatment of prisoners of war during internal armed conflicts or civil wars).

The soldiers had descended on Doramba in the morning on 17 August 2003. They were dressed in plain clothes – vests, shorts and raincoats – which concealed their weapons. Led by a major and a captain, they put the village under a lockdown and raided the house of a schoolteacher where some members of the outlawed Communist Party of Nepal (Maoist, CPN-M) were attending the wedding ceremony of two party comrades. During the raid, 19 people (17 Maoists and two civilians) were detained by the soldiers. The detainees were divided into small groups and their hands were tied behind their backs. They were ordered to march in a line and were taken to a hill outside the village. There, the detainees were executed by a firing squad. Their bodies were then thrown down the slope of the hill. Three days later, a group of Maoists came to the village and arranged the burial of their comrades – one body was buried separately by the victim's family. As the NHRC investigators discovered during the exhumation, the bodies were draped in hammer and sickle flags – for the Maoists, the victims were 'martyrs of the people's war'.[2]

The Doramba massacre – described by the RNA as an 'encounter' between the soldiers and Maoist rebels – was one of the most infamous episodes of army brutality during the decade-long civil war in Nepal. Due to the detailed nature of the NHRC investigation, it was also one of the earliest cases of RNA war crimes that attracted wide international attention – especially in countries where the royal army was seen as the benevolent saviour of Nepal, fighting against the 'Maoist menace'. For Nepalese human rights advocates, the NHRC investigation was the beginning of a campaign against encounter killings (a euphemism for extrajudicial executions, borrowed from neighbouring India) by the security forces.

The Nepalese civil war began in February 1996, as the CPN-M declared a 'people's war' against the government. The Maoists wanted to establish a 'people's republic' or 'people's democracy' by overthrowing Nepal's constitutional monarchy and replacing it with a one-party system – a system which would ostensibly guarantee a long list of human rights including women's rights, minority rights, language rights, land rights, housing rights and healthcare rights. In their war against the state, however, they themselves perpetrated war crimes and human rights abuses including: the indiscriminate bombing of civilian targets; the use of child soldiers; torture and the execution of detainees (captured government soldiers and people suspected of being RNA informers).[3]

Apart from its revolutionary goals, the 'people's war' was also a violent continuation of Nepal's struggle against the age-old monarchy – a struggle which first began in 1951 and brought an end to absolute monarchy in 1990.[4] At the same time, this insurgency in Nepal was connected to the regional 'people's war'. As part of CCOMPOSA, the umbrella organisation of revolutionary Maoist parties in South Asia, *maobadis* (Maoists) in Nepal were the Himalayan counterparts of the Naxals in India and the *sarbaharas* in Bangladesh. Within a few years, they emerged as the most successful revolutionary guerrillas in the subcontinent, while their comrades in neighbouring countries failed to gain any significant foothold that would threaten the ruling order of the state.[5]

In waging the 'people's war', the CPN-M drew its support from the people of Nepal's periphery: landless peasants, *dalits* (untouchables) and lower-caste *adivasis* (indigenous people, also known as *janajati*), who were living in abject poverty and enduring pervasive structural violence in remote villages like Doramba. The party leadership developed its military doctrine by studying the insurgency strategy of the Sendero Luminoso (Shining Path) rebels in Peru, who drew support from the indigenous peasants of the Peruvian countryside.[6] Between 1996 and 2001, while the Nepalese government maintained its control in cities and towns, the Maoists took control of the rural areas – out of 75 administrative districts in Nepal, they gained complete control of 22 districts. The writ of the central government disappeared from these areas as the rebels established a parallel government in charge of taxation, education, healthcare, criminal justice and other functions of the state. This was a textbook case of a 'protracted people's war', in which the rebels gradually took control of the periphery and prepared for a final siege of the centre.[7]

During the first phase of the 'people's war', the Nepalese government relied on the police to tackle the insurgents, as the army refused to take part in counter-insurgency operations. This was partly due to the fact that the government and the army initially did not consider the Maoist insurgency to be a serious military or political threat. The army was also reluctant to participate in an internal war under the command of a civilian administration and without the cover of a state of emergency. Then, in November 2001, the Maoists launched concerted attacks on police and army barracks across the country killing more than 80 members of the security forces. In response, the king of Nepal declared a state of emergency and deployed the army against the Maoists. As part of the new war footing, the police and the paramilitary Armed Police Force (a special counter-insurgency unit) were placed under a unified military command, which gave the army overall responsibility for counter-insurgency operations.[8]

As this was also the beginning of the 'global war on terrorism', the civil war acquired an international character when the United States, the United Kingdom and India started sponsoring the RNA through generous military aid programmes. This transformed the conflict, which until then received very little international attention, into Nepal's war on 'Maoist terrorism', a war that propelled the royal army into becoming a major counter-terrorism partner of the British and US governments.[9]

In order to ensure a free rein for the RNA in its war against the Maoists, the Nepalese king declared the state of emergency citing Article 115 of the constitution of Nepal. This declaration suspended some constitutional rights of the citizens including: freedom of expression, freedom of assembly, freedom of movement, freedom from censorship, freedom from preventive detention, the right to information, the right to property, the right to privacy and the right to judicial remedy.[10] *Habeas corpus* (a judicial safeguard against unlawful detention), however, was not suspended. The Nepalese constitution also did not indemnify or provide immunity to the security forces or government officials from eventual prosecution for abuses or misconduct during the state of emergency. This lack of immunity was seen by Nepalese national security experts as being inadequate legal protection for military commanders and soldiers, and so the army demanded the enactment of a new anti-terrorism law with explicit immunity provisions and the authorisation of extraordinary police powers.[11]

In order to satisfy this demand and to further bolster the war effort against the Maoists, the king promulgated the Terrorist and Disruptive (Control and Punishment) Ordinance (TADO) through a royal decree in 2001. In 2002, the ordinance was adopted by the Nepalese parliament as the Terrorist and Disruptive (Control and

Punishment) Act (TADA). This was a black law that provided the security forces and government officials with blanket immunity from prosecution for 'any act or work performed or attempted to be performed with bona fide motives while undertaking their duties.' The law granted the security forces draconian powers including: the preventive detention of suspected terrorists for up to six months; detention without judicial review or oversight; arbitrary arrest and detention; and warrantless search and seizure. It also provided broad and vague definitions of 'terrorism' and 'terrorist activities' which were used by the security forces for targeting suspected Maoist sympathisers including human rights advocates and lawyers defending Maoist detainees.[12]

TADO/TADA was the latest addition to a long list of security laws which granted government officials extraordinary coercive powers in the name of national security and public order. These were the Public Security Act of 1989/1991, the Local Administration Act of 1971, the Offences against State and Punishment Act of 1989 and the Public Offences Act of 1971. In order to protect 'the security or order and tranquillity of the country', the Public Security Act of 1989/1991 allowed the preventive detention of people for up to 12 months, without charge or trial. In order to maintain 'peace and security', the Local Administration Act of 1971 allowed the security forces to use lethal violence against civilians. The Offences against State and Punishment Act of 1989 and the Public Offences Act of 1971 provided vague and broad definitions of crimes such as 'disturbance', 'sedition', 'rebellion' and 'insurrection' which were used by the government for persecuting dissidents and political opponents of the monarchy.[13]

The state of emergency, TADO/TADA and other security laws equipped the army, the police and the Armed Police Force to launch a brutal campaign of terror across Nepal. Between 2001 and 2006, the security forces were responsible for more than 8,200 killings, more than 15,000 cases of arbitrary arrest/detention and more than 1,300 cases of enforced disappearance.[14] These forces also engaged in a widespread and systematic campaign of torture and murder, which took place in hundreds of torture centres that mushroomed across the country. These torture centres were invariably part of RNA barracks and outposts in cities and towns, where thousands of people were detained as suspected Maoists or Maoist sympathisers.[15]

One of the most infamous RNA torture centres identified by Nepalese and international human rights organisations was the Maharajgunj barracks in Kathmandu. In 2003, the RNA converted the barracks into an unofficial and secret detention centre for holding suspected Maoist insurgents and sympathisers, arrested from different parts of the Kathmandu valley region. The centre was jointly operated by two RNA battalions, which were responsible for counter-insurgency operations across the valley. These were the Bhairabnath battalion and the Yuddha Bhairab special operations battalion. Between 2003 and 2005, thousands of men and women were taken to the centre (known as 'Nepal's Abu Ghraib'), where they were kept continuously handcuffed and blindfolded for months. The detainees were subjected to brutal torture sessions conducted by special interrogation teams, primarily attached with the Bhairabnath battalion. These torture sessions were based on a specific regimen – used by RNA units across the country – that involved prolonged sensory deprivation; severe beating with plastic pipes; forced submersion in water (referred to as 'swimming'); electric shocks (referred to as 'ant bites') and sexual molestation.[16]

In interviews with human rights researchers and investigators, this torture regimen was later described in painful detail by the prisoners of Maharajgunj. For many of them, torture left permanent injuries. One of the prisoners related his experience in an interview with the Office of the High Commissioner for Human Rights (OHCHR, an agency of the United Nations):

I was usually taken to the tents in front of the hall where a hood was put over my head. They would ask questions before and after torture but sometimes just tortured me. They used to beat me with plastic pipes until I fell to the ground. Then someone would ask, 'What sort of ant bite would you like? Japanese or American?' The American 'bite' was higher voltage. They jabbed me with the electricity all over my body, but mostly on the soles of my feet and on my back [...] They would shove my head into filthy water that filled a big cauldron sunk into the ground. They would shove my head underwater maybe [20 or 25] times, asking me questions. Sometimes I would become unconscious. Sometimes they would punch me in the stomach when I was underwater or give me electric shocks when they pulled me up. I would feel the shock in my whole body and lose consciousness. One time I asked to urinate. They did not take me to the toilet. They took me to another spot and told me to piss. Below, I could see an electric heater coil. When I urinated, I felt the shock enter my body. I woke up much later, lying in the hall. There was saline in my arm. My genitals were swollen and painful. Later a doctor told me that I could not ever have an erection again. The damage is permanent. I heard that one person died as a result of electric shock.[17]

The brutal torture regimen adopted by the RNA indeed caused the death of hundreds of detainees across Nepal. One of the most notorious cases of torture and murder by the RNA was the killing of a 15-year-old girl, Maina Sunuwar, in Panchkhal (central Nepal). In February 2004, a group of soldiers picked up Sunuwar from her home. The soldiers were acting on a tip-off that she and her mother had ties with the Maoists. She was taken to the Birendra Peace Operations Training Centre, which was primarily used for training RNA officers before their deployment in United Nations peacekeeping missions. At the centre, Sunuwar was tortured by seven members of an army interrogation team. After forcing her to 'swim' (submersion of the head in water) for at least seven times, her interrogators repeatedly administered electric shocks to her wet hands and feet. The torture stopped only when her wrists started bleeding. Blindfolded and handcuffed, she was taken to a cell where she started foaming at the mouth and vomiting. She died within a few hours. In an attempt to cover up the murder, her body was shot several times with a M16 Colt assault rifle and secretly buried inside the training centre. Then, the commanding officer of the centre fabricated a report stating that she was killed while trying to escape from custody. It was only after the end of the war, that Sunuwar's body was exhumed by the police from a shallow grave.[18]

The torture and murder of Maina Sunuwar inside a training centre for United Nations peacekeepers drew international attention to Nepal's participation in peacekeeping missions. The case was illustrative of the peacekeeping paradox: soldiers from countries with the most unfavourable human rights records serving as UN peacekeepers, ostensibly responsible for maintaining peace and security through humanitarian interventions in many war-torn corners of the world. For troop contributing countries and their soldiers, peacekeeping missions are lucrative assignments through which they earn millions of dollars every year. In 2011, for example, the Nepalese army earned NPR6.7 billion (US$90 million) from its peacekeeping contracts with the Department of Peacekeeping Operations (DPKO) of the United Nations – this was on top of the individual salaries (more than NPR 450,000 for a six-month-long deployment) received by its soldiers.[19]

In February 2004, at the time of Sunuwar's murder, Nepal was the fifth largest troop contributor to UN peacekeeping missions, as more than 2,300 personnel of the RNA were deployed in ten missions across the globe. By the end of the year, in December 2004, Nepal became the fourth largest troop contributor, sending more than 3,400 RNA personnel to serve in 13 peacekeeping missions. In 2014, more than 5,000 Nepalese peacekeepers were serving in 15 UN-sponsored missions.[20] Many of these peacekeepers were responsible for war crimes and crimes against humanity during the Nepalese civil war. After the war, they became handsomely paid saviours of global peace (affectionately called 'Blue Helmets').[21] This was due to the failure of the DPKO to monitor and stop such individuals from joining its peacekeeping missions. Between 2006 and 2014, only two Nepalese army officers were expelled by the DPKO for their abuses during the civil war. One of them was Major Niranjan Basnet, the RNA officer responsible for the torture and murder of Maina Sunuwar at the Birendra Peace Operations Training Centre in 2004. In 2009, despite his well-documented role during the war, Basnet was deployed as a peacekeeper in Chad – it was only after an outcry from Nepalese and international human rights groups that he was expelled by the DPKO and repatriated to Nepal.[22]

Apart from his brief deployment as an UN peacekeeper, Major Niranjan Basnet had another laurel in his eventful career – he was a graduate of Sandhurst, the elite British military academy in Berkshire.[23] Like many other officers of the RNA, he received his training at the academy as part of a military assistance package through which the British government sponsored Nepal's war against the Maoists.[24] Training RNA officers at Sandhurst was only a part of the package.

Following the Nepalese government's request for help in dealing with the Maoist insurgency, the United Kingdom began training and arming the RNA in 2002. During a meeting with the Nepalese prime minister in May 2002, Tony Blair responded to this request by promising 'strong support to Nepal's fight against terrorism.'[25] Within a few months of this meeting (which took place in London), British military aid – in the form of equipment delivery and training – started flowing into Nepal.[26] Between 2002 and 2004, British security assistance to Nepal totalled GB£8.9 million.[27] During the same period, British companies supplied the RNA with weapons and ammunition (more than 6,700 assault rifles and other items) worth GB£7 million.[20] These arms export deals were readily authorised by the British government.

Between 2002 and 2005, the British government also sponsored a clandestine intelligence programme in Nepal, which targeted suspected Maoist rebels and sympathisers across the country – many of these targets were eventually detained, tortured and executed by the RNA. As part of the programme, code-named Operation Mustang, MI6 set up a 'military intelligence support group' which provided counter-insurgency and surveillance training to officers of the RNA and the National Investigation Department (NID, Nepal's national security agency). Members of the intelligence support group – MI6 officers, deployed in Kathmandu – advised the NID on techniques and strategies for infiltrating rebel networks and grooming informers. MI6 helped the NID in setting up safe houses and creating a secure radio communication network. The agency also provided the NID with cameras, computers, mobile phones and night vision binoculars. Operation Mustang, which was authorised by the British Foreign Office, continued even after the United Kingdom publicly suspended all military aid to Nepal in February 2005.[29]

British sponsorship of the RNA and NID was part of the 'global war on terrorism', proclaimed by George W. Bush and Tony Blair, following the 9/11 attacks in New York. This was despite the fact that the Nepalese Maoists did not have any ties (ideological or otherwise) with jihadist terror groups like al Qaeda. Even then, the Bush administration designated the CPN-M as a terrorist organisation and entered into a counter-terrorism alliance with the Nepalese government. For the United States, there was little or no difference between Maoist rebels and al Qaeda terrorists. As Michael Malinowski, the US ambassador to Nepal, was quoted in the New York Times in 2002: '[the Maoists] under the guise of Maoism or the so-called people's war are fundamentally the same as terrorists elsewhere – be they members of the Shining Path, Abu Sayyaf, the Khmer Rouge or al Qaeda.'[30]

Malinowski and other senior officials of the Bush administration saw the counter-insurgency campaign against the Maoists as Nepal's internal 'war on terrorism'. This was a position that propelled the United States government into becoming a major political sponsor of the Nepalese regime – especially at international forums like the United Nations Commission on Human Rights, where the United States repeatedly opposed and blocked the international condemnation of human rights abuses by the RNA and other security forces. Maintaining a double standard, the United States refrained from condemning the war crimes and crimes against humanity perpetrated by the RNA, while routinely condemning human rights abuses perpetrated by 'Maoist terrorists'.[31]

Apart from diplomatic sponsorship, the United States was also a major military sponsor of the RNA – providing weapons, services and training to the royal army through generous military aid programmes.[32] Between 2002 and 2004, the United States supplied the RNA with a steady flow of weapons, including more than 20,000 M16 assault rifles, which became the standard-issue weapon for Nepalese counter-insurgency troops. The United States also equipped these counter-insurgency troops with M14 carbines, grenade launchers, body armour, night vision goggles and communication devices. As part of military aid, Nepal also received high-tech counter-insurgency hardware and Huey II helicopters which would ensure 'improved mobility' for the RNA.

A major component of the United States' military aid to the RNA was training under the IMET (International Military Education and Training) programme, described by the Department of State as 'an instrument of US national security and foreign policy'.[33] Between 2002 and 2004, hundreds of RNA officers attended IMET-sponsored training sessions – worth more than US$1.5 million – conducted inside special military facilities in both Nepal and the United States. These sessions were tailor-made for the RNA and oriented specifically towards intelligence gathering, psychological warfare and special operations targeting the Maoist insurgency. During the same period, RNA officers also attended joint training exercises with United States Special Forces under the JCET (Joint Combined Exchange Training) programme. As part of JCET, military experts and special forces troops routinely travelled to Nepal and held joint special operations training sessions.

The United States coordinated its military aid efforts in Nepal with India – one of the two regional hegemons (the other being China) and the staunchest political sponsor of the Nepalese regime. Nepal had been an Indian client state for many years.[34] Since the beginning of the civil war, the Indian government consistently maintained that the conflict between the Nepalese government and the CPN-M was Nepal's 'internal matter'. As this ostensibly fell under Nepal's domestic jurisdiction, India actively opposed any role for the United Nations and other international organisations in monitoring the conflict, even when the RNA was perpetrating war crimes and crimes against humanity in clear violation of international humanitarian law and human rights law. This Indian position was partly influenced by India's own counter-insurgency campaigns or internal wars in Kashmir and the north-eastern states. Indian national security experts were also concerned about the CPN-M's ties with Naxals and other Maoist groups in India. Without concrete evidence, some of these experts also accused China and Pakistan of sponsoring the Maoists.

India had been one of the major suppliers of weapons to Nepal, even before the onset of the civil war. Since 2001, Indian military aid to Nepal increased significantly.[35] However, details about Indian aid packages delivered to Nepal remain sketchy, given the secretive nature of India's military cooperation programmes, especially with its neighbours. In April 2003, a senior official of the Indian Army revealed that India provided Nepal with weapons and ammunition worth US$25.8 million – he also revealed that India was planning to deliver more weapons and ammunition worth US$12.9 million. Apart from this massive arms transfer, the Indian Army provided counter-insurgency training to hundreds of RNA officers during the civil war. Indeed, in its crackdown against the Maoists, the RNA used the same tools of terror (like encounter killings) that were first developed and deployed by Indian death squads (Assam Rifles, CRPF and Rashtriya Rifles) in the seven sister states, Punjab and Kashmir. For many Indian national security experts, Nepal's war against the Maoists was an extension of India's own war against revolutionary Naxal groups.

The civil war and international sponsorship of the Nepalese national security machinery by India, the United States and the United Kingdom fundamentally transformed Nepal's military economy.[36] Before the civil war, Nepal had one of the smallest armies in Asia, sponsored through a small military budget. In 2000, a year before the RNA started participating in counter-insurgency operations, Nepal had a military budget of NPR3.5 billion (US$50 million) for sustaining 46,000 troops of the RNA. By 2004, this budget had shot up to NPR8 billion (US$110 million). In 2005, the budget was further raised to NPR10.5 billion (US$151 million). In 2006, the last year of the war, there were 69,000 troops in the RNA and 15,000 paramilitary troops in the Armed Police Force. Before the civil war, Nepalese soldiers and regular policemen were among the most under-equipped security forces in the world. Due to the generous supply from foreign sponsors, they had been equipped with some of the deadliest counter-insurgency weapons during the civil war – weapons which they deployed in terror campaigns against their own people, including 15-year-old children.

Despite the terror campaigns carried out by the RNA and imposition of a new state of emergency in February 2005, Nepal's monarchy crumbled in May 2006. The Maoists failed to establish their desired 'people's republic' but succeeded in overthrowing the monarchy by entering into an alliance with seven pro-democracy political parties. In a curious turn of events, the violent Maoist insurgency transformed into a mass movement for democracy – loktantra andolan – in the Spring of 2006.[37] In November 2006, the civil war ended with the signing of a peace agreement between the CPN-M and a new Nepalese government led by pro-democracy politicians. Nepal finally became a democratic republic, after officially abolishing the 240-year-old monarchy on 28 May 2008.[38] In many ways, it was also the day the RNA-led national security state was formally defeated by Nepalese human rights advocates. Since then, they have embarked on a new campaign, demanding justice for the victims of crimes against humanity committed by the RNA and the CPN-M during the civil war – a campaign that led to the arrest of Colonel Kumar Lama in the United Kingdom and the expulsion of Major Niranjan Basnet from the peacekeeping mission in Chad.

Among the five national security states in South Asia, Nepal is the only country that was never a part of the British Raj – a distinction that sets it apart from its neighbours, especially in terms of military capacity. At the onset of the civil war, the Nepalese regime indeed had the weakest and least-developed military machinery in the region (ranking only above Bhutan).[39] Even to this day, despite the scars of the civil war, the Himalayan nation remains one of the two least-militarised societies in the subcontinent (the other being Bhutan) – a society that is now slowly emerging as a rare beacon of democracy and freedom, albeit struggling through post-war political crises.[40] It is against this backdrop that Nepalese human rights organisations and civil society groups are now seeking truth and reconciliation – the success or failure of their campaign will determine if the death squads will ever return to Doramba, Kathmandu or Panchkhal.[41]

5

PAKISTAN: AGENTS OF THE STATE

1. Saleem Badini – disappeared in December 2011 – body found in January 2012
2. Wazir Khan Marri – disappeared in September 2011 – body found in January 2012
20. Sangat Sana Baloch – disappeared in December 2009 body found in February 2012
27. Raheem Dad Nichari – disappeared in December 2011 – body found in February 2012
30. Abdul Ghaffar – disappeared in February 2012 – body found in March 2012
57. Unidentified – date of disappearance unknown – body found in May 2012

> Bodies of missing persons found in Balochistan in 2012, HRCP fact-finding mission report[1]

Just a few weeks before his abduction, Sangat Sana Baloch was looking for volunteers who would help the Baloch Republican Party (BRP) with its official website. He posted messages in different online forums asking for help with web development and report writing. 'We appreciate any minute contribution,' he wrote. Baloch was a dedicated party worker, well known for his fiery speeches calling for independence of Balochistan. In December 2009, he was abducted by Pakistani security forces in north-western Balochistan – after 798 days, in February 2012, his mutilated dead body, with marks of torture and bullet wounds, was found near the city of Turbat in southern Balochistan.[2] The BRP website now hosts a photo of the body. There are more than 160 photos, depicting cases of enforced disappearance and extrajudicial execution of party workers. The party describes them as martyred freedom fighters in the struggle for an *azad* (independent) Balochistan.

The western province of Balochistan in Pakistan is the largest of its four provinces, covering 44 per cent of the country's land mass. It is also the least populated province, with only 5 per cent of the total population of the country. The province is home to some of the poorest citizens of Pakistan – more than 60 per cent residents of Balochistan live below the poverty line.[3] The eastern part of the province has large deposits of natural resources: oil, gas, copper and gold. Control over this remote corner of the province is one of the major reasons behind the ongoing conflict between the government of Pakistan and Baloch nationalists, who want control over their own homeland and the resources buried underneath. This is a conflict that has turned the province into a militarised zone, where thousands of Pakistani troops are now engaged in a brutal internal war. For Pakistani security forces deployed in Balochistan, this war is about safeguarding the territorial integrity of the state – for Baloch nationalists, on the other hand, this is a war of independence.[4] This Baloch struggle for an *azad* Balochistan is of course very similar to the Kashmiri struggle for an *azad* Kashmir, and there are eerie similarities between the campaigns of state terror carried out by Pakistani and Indian security forces.[5]

Since the end of the British Raj in 1947, Baloch nationalists have been opposing and challenging Pakistan's occupation and rule of their homeland, mostly through peaceful and non-violent means. Some separatist groups, however, have been waging armed insurgencies against the state of Pakistan. In response, Pakistani security forces have been carrying out counter-insurgency operations in the province since 1958. The latest round of counter-insurgency operations were launched in 2005. Since then, as part of these operations, the security forces have been perpetrating horrific human rights abuses across the province: torture, extrajudicial execution, enforced disappearance, the use of lethal force against civilians and the forced displacement of civilians.[6]

The primary victims of torture, extrajudicial execution and enforced disappearance are members of Baloch nationalist parties and movements: the Baloch Republican Party (BRP), the Baloch Nationalist Front (BNF), the Baloch National Movement (BNM), the Balochistan National Party (BNP) and the Baloch Student Organization (BSO-Azad). Hundreds of Baloch activists are abducted every year and tortured to death. Their mutilated bodies are then dumped by the roadside in cities, towns and villages across the province.[7] According to Pakistani and international human rights organisations, the victims are most often abducted by groups of armed men who usually arrive in unmarked four-door pick-up vans.[8] These armed men are from the intelligence agencies: the Directorate for Inter-Services Intelligence (ISI), Military Intelligence (MI) and the Intelligence Bureau (IB). In a large number of cases, the paramilitary Frontier Corps (FC) also carries out counter-insurgency raids against suspected members of Baloch organisations – abducting, torturing and executing them.[9]

Torture, enforced disappearance and extrajudicial execution by the security forces have also been rampant in the southern province of Sindh. Here, the primary targets are political activists affiliated with different Sindh-based parties and movements. Human rights groups and Sindhi organisations have held the intelligence agencies and paramilitary Pakistan Rangers responsible for most of the cases of abuse against Sindhi activists.[10] A secondary group of targets are the lumpenproletariat of Karachi – the provincial capital of Sindh and Pakistan's commercial capital. Like Mumbai in India, Karachi is home to millions of internal migrants and immigrants (from Afghanistan, India, Bangladesh) who live in the city's slum districts.[11] Some of the most notorious crime gangs of Pakistan are based in these slums. Members of these gangs frequently become the victims of torture and extrajudicial execution (euphemistically described as 'encounter') carried out by encounter squads of the police and Pakistan Rangers.[12]

In another region of Pakistan, in the north-western province of Khyber Pakhtunkhwa (erstwhile North-West Frontier Province), the Pakistan Army has been carrying out counter-insurgency operations against the militants of Tehrik-e-Taliban Pakistan (TTP) – also known as the Pakistani Taliban, an umbrella organisation of at least 13 Islamist groups engaged in a *jihad* (holy war) against the government of Pakistan.[13] Establishing the rule of *sharia* (Islamic law), defeating the US-led NATO/ISAF forces in Afghanistan and destroying the Pakistan Army are the three key goals of these groups. Most of these groups are currently active in Khyber Pakhtunkhwa as well as other provinces including Balochistan and Sindh.

The TTP was founded by the Taliban commander Baitullah Mehsud in December 2007. The current leader of the organisation is Mullah Fazlullah, the alleged mastermind behind a gruesome massacre at a school that shocked the world in December 2014. The massacre took place at the Army Public School in the city of Peshawar, the provincial capital of Khyber Pakhtunkhwa. On 16 December, seven TTP gunmen raided the school and indiscriminately gunned down the staff and children – more than 145 were killed, among them at least 132 were schoolchildren.[14] Most of them were the children of army officers. The siege of the school ended with a rescue operation by Pakistani special forces who killed the gunmen and rescued at least 960 people, many of them with serious injuries. This was the deadliest terrorist attack in the history of Pakistan. The TTP officially claimed responsibility for the massacre within hours of the attack, describing it as a revenge for Operation Zarb-e-Azb, a counter-insurgency crackdown launched by the army in June 2014.[15]

The army had launched Operation Zarb-e-Azb in response to a TTP attack on Jinnah International Airport in Karachi (in Sindh) – at least 23 people, including TTP militants, were killed during the attack on the airport.[16] During the retaliatory crackdown which first began in North Waziristan (in north-western Pakistan), the army deployed armoured battalions, air support units, drones and more than 30,000 troops. This was one of the largest Pakistani offensives against the TTP since 2009. Between June 2014 and December 2014, the security forces killed more than 1,200 TTP insurgents.[17] The offensive displaced about one million civilians in the region.[18] During the siege of the Army Public School in Peshawar, the TTP gunmen were avenging the killings of their brethren by slaughtering the children of army officers. This, indeed, was the rationale behind the massacre.

As part of its counter-insurgency operations in Khyber Pakhtunkhwa, the army has engaged in systematic campaigns of abuses – torture and extrajudicial execution of suspected TTP insurgents. In the Swat valley region of the province, the army carried out more than 238 extrajudicial executions between 2009 and 2010.[19] In most of these cases, the victims – suspected TTP insurgents – died in army custody. Their bodies were later found with bullet wounds and marks of torture. These bodies were dumped by the roadside in towns and villages across the valley. In some cases, the bullet-ridden bodies were left hanging from utility poles with warning messages pinned on them, 'Anyone who joins the Taliban will meet the same fate.'[20] Pakistani human rights groups also confirmed the existence of 'mass graves stuffed with dead bodies of the Taliban' – many residents of Swat valley, traumatised by TTP atrocities in the region, approved of these killings.[21]

While Pakistani intelligence agencies and security forces have engaged in systematic campaigns of abduction, torture and execution targeting different groups of insurgents in different regions of the country, the national security machinery of Pakistan has also targeted intellectuals – journalists, writers, academics and artists – for persecution. Intellectuals who are seen as troublesome or threatening to the national security establishment are routinely subjected to sinister harassments, threats and attacks by the security agencies. And, in some cases, they become victims of enforced disappearance, torture, execution or assassination.[22]

One such case was the abduction and murder of the journalist Saleem Shahzad, a correspondent of the Italian news agency Adnkronos International and the Pakistan bureau chief for Asia Times Online. Shahzad was best known for his authoritative reporting about Pakistan's military and its ties with Islamist militants including al Qaeda operatives. In May 2011, he published an article holding an al Qaeda cell responsible for a commando attack on Pakistan's main naval base in Karachi. The article detailed how Pakistani military personnel provided the attackers with maps and logistical information. This exposé was embarrassing for the military, that had always denied maintaining any ties with al Qaeda or other Islamist terror groups.

A few days after the article was published, Shahzad was abducted from Islamabad – the Pakistani capital – on 29 May 2011. He was on his way to a television studio, to participate in a talk show. The following day, his body was found in a canal near the city of Mandi Bahauddin, 150 kilometres south-east of Islamabad. The body had external and internal signs of brutal torture – 17 wounds from a blunt instrument; ruptured liver and two broken ribs. At the time of his death, Shahzad was 40 years old. According to the Committee to Protect Journalists, he was the 37th Pakistani journalist killed since September 2001.

According to evidence gathered by intelligence officials in the United States and Human Rights Watch (HRW) researchers, Saleem Shahzad was abducted and then tortured to death by the Directorate for Inter-Services Intelligence (ISI). Before his abduction, Shahzad informed the Pakistan director of HRW about threats he had received from senior military officers during a meeting at the ISI headquarters. After his abduction, HRW was able to confirm that he indeed was in ISI custody.[23] Then, in July 2011, US government officials held the ISI responsible for his abduction and murder. As one of the officials told the *New York Times*, 'Every indication is that this was a deliberate, targeted killing that was most likely meant to send shock waves through Pakistan's journalist community and civil society.'[24]

The official, of course, did not say anything about the United States' role in bolstering the Pakistani national security state, of which the ISI is one of the principal organs. Very few government officials in Washington will ever admit on record that the United States is the chief international sponsor of Pakistan's state terror machinery. Indeed, the United States emerged as the biggest military and economic backer of Pakistan since its independence in 1947 – between 1951 and 2011, the United States pledged US$67 billion to Pakistan in military and economic aid.[25]

The two countries were strong military allies during the Cold War. Even in 1971, as the Pakistan Army was slaughtering Bengalis in East Pakistan, the United States was firm in its support for its ally and continued delivering military aid.[26] Between 1951 and 1991, the United States bankrolled Pakistan with millions of aid dollars. This was also the period when the first and second generations of Pakistani military rulers were developing the national security state, especially after the secession of East Pakistan and during the rule of General Zia-ul-Haq. The general was Ronald Reagan's 'frontline ally' in his fight against Soviet communism.[27]

After the Cold War, the massive inflow of US aid into Pakistan virtually stopped between 1992 and 2001 – the official reason for this halt was Pakistan's nuclear weapons programme. This, roughly, was also the period when the governments of Benazir Bhutto and Nawaz Sharif were struggling to re-establish the democratic order in the country.

In a post-9/11 world, as George W. Bush launched his 'global war on terrorism' in Afghanistan, US aid dollars once again started flowing into Pakistan. This time there was a new military dictator in charge of the country – General Pervez Musharraf, who overthrew the democratic government of Nawaz Sharif in October 1999. Between 2002 and 2009, the United States poured millions of aid dollars into Pakistan – 70 per cent of this was military aid and 30 per cent was economic aid.[28] In 2004, George W. Bush designated Pakistan as a major non-NATO ally. In that same year, a new National Security Council was established in Pakistan. By 2011, Pakistan had become the fourth largest recipient of US aid – after Israel, Afghanistan and Egypt.[29]

One of the building blocks of the renewed partnership between the United States and Pakistan was a US-sponsored counter-insurgency programme. According to a report by the Congressional Research Service, the programme was the brainchild of Department of Defense officials who were frustrated by the 'feckless counter-insurgency efforts of the internally squabbling Islamabad government.'[30] In order to assist Pakistan 'in reorienting its army for counter-insurgency efforts', the Department of Defense proposed the creation of a dedicated Pakistan Counter-insurgency Fund (PCF) – this fund was approved by the United States Congress and later renamed as Pakistan Counter-insurgency Capability Fund (PCCF). Between 2009 and 2012, the United States disbursed US$661 million through PCF/PCCF, to sponsor Pakistan's counter-insurgency operations.[31]

Between 2001 and 2013, Pakistan also received US$10.7 billion for participating in US-led counter-terrorism operations. This came from the special Coalition Support Funds (CSF). Payments from CSF were used for sponsoring more than 100,000 Pakistani troops in north-western Pakistan – paying for their food, clothing, housing and ammunition. These funds were also used for supplying Pakistan with 26 utility helicopters. Through another special fund called Section 1206, the United States also supplied Pakistan with four helicopters; four surveillance aircrafts; 450 vehicles for the Frontier Corps; 20 explosive detection and disposal vehicles; night vision devices and other counter-insurgency hardware. In 2007, the Department of Defense started training and equipping the Frontier Corps using its own funds.[32]

Indeed, the wide proliferation of enforced disappearances in Pakistan was a by-product of the US-led 'global war on terrorism'. Since 2001, Pakistani security agencies – especially the ISI – had abducted hundreds of suspected al Qaeda members and held them in secret detention facilities across the country. Many of these detainees were handed over to the United States without any judicial supervision or review. This, in effect, was bounty hunting – an extremely lucrative business in trading suspected terrorists for cash. As General Pervez Musharraf noted in his autobiography:

> We have captured 689 and handed over 369 to the United States. We have earned bounties totalling millions of dollars. Those who habitually accuse us of 'not doing enough' in the war on terror should simply ask the CIA how much prize money it has paid to the government of Pakistan.[33]

These, of course, were the first batch of detainees processed through the new counter-insurgency machinery of Pakistan. And the United

States was not the only Western country that benefited from this machinery. Pakistan had another counter-terrorism partner – the United Kingdom.

Between 2004 and 2007, the United Kingdom was an eager buyer of information that Pakistani security agencies obtained through systematic use of torture at secret detention facilities. In effect, the Pakistanis tortured and interrogated terrorism suspects on behalf of British intelligence agencies. This was the case for British citizens detained in Pakistan on suspicion of terrorism. These detainees were held at secret facilities where they were subjected to brutal torture sessions while Pakistani interrogators – from the ISI, MI and IB – questioned them about their presumed ties with al Qaeda and other terror groups. They were asked specific questions which were given to their Pakistani interrogators by British MI6 and MI5 agents. In some cases, their torture was followed by a visit from British officials. These cases were rigorously investigated and documented by British journalists and international human rights groups.[34]

One of the British citizens who survived torture by the ISI was Rangzieb Ahmed, detained in August 2006. Ahmed later described his experience to Human Rights Watch:

I was repeatedly hit with a stick and a weapon made from the tread of a tire and fixed to a stick at one end. I was beaten with a stick on the soles of my feet. They would push me to the floor and pull my feet up on to a chair and hold them there while they hit the soles of my feet with the stick. I was also beaten around the head and on my arms with the stick. The weapon made from a tire was used to beat me on my buttocks. I was also hit with an electrical cable. During this period, especially in the first five days, I was not allowed to sleep. The interrogators woke me up and threatened to chain me to the door to prevent me sleeping when they saw me falling asleep.

The interrogation room was monitored with cameras though I could not tell if they just recorded or allowed others to watch the interrogation as it happened. I believe the interrogations were definitely monitored because slips of paper would be brought into the room with messages that seemed like questions or advice for the interrogators. ...

I was held down on the ground by five of them. One used pliers to pull a fingernail from my left hand. They would pull a bit of the nail out, ask me questions and then inject me with painkillers for temporary relief. Then the questions and the pulling would begin again. This went on for eight days. Over this period, they completely pulled out three fingernails from the little finger, my ring finger and my middle finger of the left hand. ...

[Sometime in September 2006,] British officials came and questioned me, they said they were from the British government, not the embassy. They showed me photos of people they wanted me to identify.[35]

The torture of British citizens in Pakistani custody represented globalisation of a sinister variety, in which Western national security states outsourced their torture needs to other national security states in the periphery of the world capitalist system. The prime example which illustrated the globalisation of torture – also known as torture by proxy – was extraordinary rendition. This was a process pioneered by the United States, in which terrorism suspects were illegally transferred to Third World national security states for processing through a network of secret detention facilities and torture chambers – also known as black sites.[36]

The United Kingdom and the United States are not the only sponsors of state terror in Pakistan. After the United States, China is Pakistan's strongest security partner and military ally. As Asif Ali Zardari, former president of Pakistan, once wrote in an article, 'No relationship between two sovereign states is as unique and durable as that between Pakistan and China.'[37] Indeed, China has been one of the key political sponsors of Pakistan, especially at the United Nations. In 1971, when the Pakistan Army was perpetrating a genocide in East Pakistan, the Chinese delegation at the United Nations Security Council was busy defending Pakistan's sovereign right to deal with its internal matters, and denouncing India for supporting separatist Bengali insurgents.[38] In December 1971, when Zulfikar Ali Bhutto – Asif Ali Zardari's father-in-law – addressed the Security Council defending Pakistani atrocities, Chinese and US diplomats were his closest allies present in the chamber.[39]

China has emerged as Pakistan's largest military supplier and strongest regional ally since the Sino-Indian war of 1962. Since then, China has supplied Pakistan with weapons worth millions of dollars: combat aircraft, warships, helicopters, tanks, small arms, light weapons and ammunition. Pakistan also produces weapons and ammunition in its ordnance factories using Chinese technology and production licences. China is also financing the construction of a deep-sea port near the city of Gwadar in Balochistan. The port would secure the supply of oil and gas from the Persian Gulf to China and could also become a strategic base for Chinese warships in the Indian Ocean region. The Chinese policy of arming Pakistan through a steady flow of weapons is partly influenced by its strategic interests in tilting the military balance against India, the other big power in the region.[40]

Since its independence, Pakistan has recurrently found itself at the centre of major geopolitical struggles between big powers. During the Cold War, the country became a strategic asset for the United States, as successive US presidents used their ties with Pakistani military dictators to challenge Soviet interests in the region, especially in Afghanistan. Pakistan also became a Chinese asset in its strategic manoeuvres against India. Then, after the Cold War, in a post-9/11 world, another Pakistani military dictator became a major US–UK ally in the 'war against terrorism' – an ally who also hired out detention facilities and torture chambers.

These ties and partnerships transcended ideological boundaries. Neither ideology nor ethical/moral standards were impediments to international sponsorship of Pakistan's terror – Pakistan was an ally of the capitalist United States in its battles against the communist Soviet Union; Pakistan was an ally of communist China in its battles against democratic India; Pakistan, the Islamic Republic, was a major US ally in its war against Islamic terrorism; Pakistan tortured British citizens at the behest of British security officials.

Pakistan's ruling elite and its military leaders used these ties and partnerships to bolster the Pakistani national security state and to bankroll its campaigns of state terror in East Pakistan, Balochistan, Sindh and Khyber Pakhtunkhwa. These campaigns of terror were primarily sponsored or authorised through proclamations of martial law, declarations of state of emergency and the enactment of national security laws or black laws – proclamations, declarations and laws that created states of exception in the new colonies and disturbed areas of Pakistan, where the agents and soldiers of the state perpetrated horrific abuses with absolute impunity.

The latest versions of Pakistan's black laws include the Anti-Terrorism Act (ATA) of 1997 and Protection of Pakistan Act (PPA) of 2014. Human rights groups have identified the ATA as the key piece of legislation that facilitates the enforced disappearance (secret detention) of suspected insurgents, especially in Balochistan.[41] The PPA, on the other hand, is the key piece of legislation that is now being used by the national security bureaucracy for sponsoring internal wars and deploying military and paramilitary forces as part of these wars.[42]

The Pakistani national security state has been sustained through colossal military budgets, at the expense of ordinary Pakistanis. In 2013, Pakistan had a military budget of PKR573 billion (US$6 billion) – this was 3.5 per cent of GDP and 19.5 per cent of central government expenditure.[43] In 2014, the budget shot up to PKR632 billion (US$6.31 billion) – then, in 2015, the budget was raised to PKR703 billion (US$6.96 billion).[44] This budget is for maintaining a massive network of armed forces, paramilitary forces, national security agencies, defence colleges and branches of the ministry of defence. Since 2008, the military budget has been oriented more towards covering Pakistan's war effort against its internal enemies and more money is being put into counter-insurgency operations in Balochistan and Khyber Pakhtunkhwa.[45]

Pakistan has one of the largest militaries in South Asia. There are more than 643,000 active soldiers and commanders in its armed forces: 550,000 in the army, 70,000 in the air force and 23,800 in the navy.[46] The army is divided into at least 22 divisions (15,000–

25,000 combat troops), 34 independent brigades (3,000–5,000 combat troops) and 17 special squadrons. Of these, three divisions and two independent brigades are deployed in Balochistan while two divisions and one independent brigade are deployed in Khyber Pakhtunkhwa.

In these areas, the army's counter-insurgency operations against Baloch nationalists and TTP insurgents are supported by 65,000 paramilitary troops of the Frontier Corps, deployed in 40 battalions across the provinces.[47] More than 40,000 paramilitary troops of the Pakistan Rangers are deployed in Sindh and Punjab (Pakistan's core and most populous province).[48] These forces are invariably commanded by generals deputed from the Pakistan Army. Like the Assam Rifles in India, these two paramilitary forces were originally raised by the British colonial rulers to control the peripheral regions of the Raj. The Frontier Corps was created by Lord Curzon (the then Viceroy) in 1907, as he combined seven different militias responsible for controlling different tribal agencies bordering Afghanistan.[49] The Pakistan Rangers, on the other hand, was raised by the British in 1942 as the Sindh Police Rifles (later renamed Sindh Police Rangers).[50] In their post-colonial incarnations, both forces now operate as paramilitary death squads.

Pakistan's dirty war against its internal enemies – separatists, insurgents and troublesome journalists – is conducted by military and civilian intelligence agencies. These are the death squads of the national security state: the Directorate for Inter-Services Intelligence (ISI), Military Intelligence (MI) and the Intelligence Bureau (IB). Among these, the ISI is the most notorious for its dirty ops (covert operations) in Pakistan as well as in neighbouring countries like India and Bangladesh. The agency was created by Major General Robert Cawthome, a British-Australian officer of the British Indian Army who stayed back in newly independent Pakistan to serve in the newly formed Pakistan Army.[51] Between 1959 and 1969, the agency first emerged as one of the principal organs of the national security state under the patronage of Field Marshal Ayub Khan, the first military dictator of Pakistan.[52]

Ayub Khan's successor General Yahya Khan was the earliest proponent of establishing a National Security Council in Pakistan, modelled after the National Security Council in the United States. Since 1977, Yahya Khan's successors had continued to advocate the establishment of such a council, modelled after the military-dominated council in Turkey. In Pakistan, the council would ensure the military and its commanders a permanent role in governance of the country – granting them membership of the ruling elite. As a permanent organ of the government, it would institutionalise the military's control over the politics of security. In other words, the National Security Council would be a device of governance and policymaking through which Pakistan's specialists on violence would ensure their dominance over the larger society. The military, however, failed in its attempts to establish a permanent National Security Council until 2004, when General Pervez Musharraf was finally able to establish the council through parliamentary legislation. With the return of democracy in Pakistan, the Cabinet Committee on National Security (previously known as the Defence Committee of Cabinet) replaced the National Security Council as the government's principal policymaking organ on security matters. The committee is led by the civilian prime minister and dominated by senior military and intelligence leaders.[53]

These military and intelligence leaders – Pakistan's specialists on violence – are also the stewards of another institution known as Milbus or 'Military Inc'. This is an elaborate and ever-expansive system that guarantees the military's position as the predominant class in Pakistani society, through the creation and maintenance of an independent military economy. In effect, it is a system of economic exploitation through which resources and opportunities are transferred from ordinary Pakistanis to their saviours in the barracks.[54]

In this system, Pakistan's specialists on violence have become powerful economic actors as they embark on large-scale business ventures across the country: fertilizer, cement and cereal manufacturing plants; radio and television stations; commercial banks; insurance companies; agribusinesses; hotels and resorts; airlines;

real estate development and hundreds of other ventures in the private sector.[55] Indeed, the military in Pakistan is not only the saviour of the country but also one of its largest and most influential corporations. This system also involves providing active and retired military officers and their families with special perks and privileges: membership of exclusive clubs and other leisure facilities; subsidies on utility bills; the subsidised import of vehicles for personal use by officers; elite schools and colleges for officers' children; exclusive residential areas for retired officers and hundreds of other perks and privileges that make the military the most pampered class in Pakistan.[56]

The national security state in Pakistan (also known as the 'deep state' or 'state within state') is the prime example of a repressive system administered by specialists on violence and sponsored by global and regional hegemons. Since 1958, Pakistan's military rulers have not only embarked on dirty wars against internal enemies in Balochistan, East Pakistan, Sindh and Khyber Pakhtunkhwa but have also transformed their country into a garrison-state-for-rent, by selling their services in violence and brutality to eager customers – trading detainees with the CIA and torturing terrorism suspects on behalf of MI5 and MI6. In exchange for generous military aid from the United States and China, they had also transformed Pakistan into a bulwark or deterrent against the Soviet Union (during the Cold War), the Taliban (post 9/11) and India (since 1962). Military aid from the United States and China has paid for Pakistan's machinery of repression: counter insurgency forces, intelligence agencies, secret detention facilities and torture chambers. This indeed is the machinery that is now being used by agents of the national security state for eliminating political activists and dissident intellectuals across the country.

6

SRI LANKA: WHITE VANS

The long war that went on for nearly three decades was over and Sri Lankans across the globe were celebrating. This jubilation was especially strong and visible in London, given the large size of the Sri Lankan diaspora in the United Kingdom.[1] This was in May 2009, a few days after the defeat of the LTTE (Liberation Tigers of Tamil Eelam) rebels. On 23 May, hundreds of British-Sri Lankans and a large group of Buddhist monks gathered at the Kingsbury *Vihara* (monastery) in north-west London. They were attending a *Bodhi puja* (holy ritual involving the sacred Bodhi tree).[2]

The *puja* was organised for blessing 'all the war heroes' of Sri Lanka. The heroes were Mahinda Rajapaksa (president), Keheliya Rambukwella (defence and national security spokesman), Lieutenant Colonel Gotabaya Rajapaksa (secretary of defence and brother of the president), General Sarath Fonseka (commander of the army), Admiral Wasantha Karannagoda (commander of the navy), Air Chief Marshal Roshan Goonetileke (commander of the air force), Jayantha Wickramaratne (inspector general of the police) and 'all the service men and women of the security forces who [were] rendering great service for the integrity of the motherland.' The Sri Lankan High Commissioner to the United Kingdom, Nehal Jayasinghe, attended the event on their behalf.

The High Commissioner distributed saffron robes to the monks while other devotees gave alms. Then, senior monks conducted the *puja* and delivered their sermons. One of the monks, Handupelpola Mahinda Nayaka, extolled President Rajapaksa in his sermon for showing the world 'the real way to fight terrorism' and offered his blessings, 'We wish our brave soldiers and their [commander-in-chief] good health and long life, so that they can save Sri Lanka and its people...' The *puja* ended with the monks chanting *paritta* (verses of protection).

Saving Sri Lanka by defeating the separatist LTTE rebels was no mean feat. The Sri Lankan civil war was an ethnic conflict between the Tamil militants of the LTTE and the Sinhalese-dominated government forces.[3] The war had ravaged the island country since 1983 – it was one of the deadliest armed conflicts in recent history. According to estimates by the United Nations, 80,000–100,000 had been killed since the beginning of the conflict; more than 136,000 Sri Lankans became refugees and more than 440,000 had been displaced from their homes – the exact numbers, however, could be much higher.[4]

The conflict came to a brutal end when the Sri Lankan forces ferociously attacked LTTE-held territories in northern Sri Lanka. The army captured and killed the notorious LTTE commander Velupillai Prabhakaran on 18 May 2009. When the news of his death reached Colombo, thousands of Sri Lankans came out on the streets of the capital to party, carrying the maroon-yellow national flag. Some of them were also carrying effigies of Prabhakaran.[5]

On 19 March, President Rajapaksa gave his victory speech to the parliament. 'Our motherland has been completely freed from the clutches of separatist terrorism. From now on only the laws enacted by this sovereign parliament will be in force in every inch of Sri Lanka,' he declared before a full house.[6] Then, on 3 June, he led a victory parade in Colombo. It was a grand event attended by thousands of soldiers and their civilian supporters. As the celebrations went on in Colombo and other major cities, thousands of Tamil civilians remained interned in hundreds of makeshift camps in northern Sri Lanka. They had been displaced from their homes during the final phase of the battle between the Sri Lankan forces and the LTTE.

During this final battle, the civilians were subjected to horrific war crimes from both sides.[7] The Sri Lankan army killed thousands of them with indiscriminate and relentless shelling while the LTTE used them as human shields. Most of these civilians died inside the 'no fire zone' of Vanni, which was set up to provide humanitarian protection to people fleeing from the war. The army not only shelled the 'no fire zone' with heavy artillery, it also cut off the supply lines used by humanitarian agencies for distributing food, water and medicine. The army also attacked and destroyed hospitals and medical camps in LTTE-held areas.

As the army took complete control of LTTE-held areas in northern Sri Lanka, surrendering LTTE rebels were subjected to extrajudicial executions. Hundreds of rebels were shot dead; female LTTE members were raped before they were killed. Photographs of these massacres showed rows of dead bodies – blindfolded and with their hands tied behind their backs. Most of these executions were carried out by the 58 Division of the army. The division was under the command of Brigadier Shavendra Silva. Eyewitnesses later confirmed that Silva was acting on direct orders from Gotabaya Rajapaksa, the secretary of defence. One of the eyewitnesses also described how the 58 Division targeted Tamil civilians:

They shot people at random. Stabbed people. Raped them. Cut out their tongues, cut women's breasts off. I have witnessed this with my own eyes. I saw the naked dead bodies of women without heads and other parts of their bodies. I saw a lot of small, innocent children getting killed in large numbers. I saw people soaked in blood.[8]

All of these were terrible violations of the laws of war. Even then, for many Sri Lankans (including some Buddhist monks), members of the security forces and their commanders were war heroes who showed the world the real way to fight terrorism. The *Bodhi puja* in London was of course held in the name of Buddha. However, it was dedicated to the gods of national security back in Sri Lanka – the real saviours of the motherland.

The national security state in Sri Lanka developed against the backdrop of the civil war. This was the result of an active partnership between political leaders and military commanders. Since 1983, the island had been under a state of emergency as the office of the president and the parliament churned out emergency regulations and anti-terrorism laws. These laws not only suspended the civil and political rights of the citizens but also turned the military into a de facto government. With the establishment of a National Security Council in 1999, the centre of power gradually moved from the parliament to the military barracks.[9]

It was in this context that worshipping war heroes became a regular ritual in the temple of national security. Even traditional religious rituals – like *Bodhi puja* or *paritta* chanting – were militarised in the service of war.[10] The new religion of national security had its own symbol, not the sacred Bodhi tree but the sinister white van. The unmarked white van was the vehicle of choice for the priests of state terror – military, paramilitary and police death squads.

In June 2009, a few weeks after the end of the war, an unidentified group of armed men used one of these vans to abduct the journalist Poddala Jayantha in Colombo. He was one of the staunchest press freedom advocates in Sri Lanka. As the secretary of the Sri Lanka Working Journalists' Association (SLWJA), he was a vocal critic of the Rajapaksa government and its draconian treatment of journalists. As a reporter, he wrote about the corruption in the military and the rights of the Tamil people.

After abducting him from the streets, Jayantha's captors tortured him for hours and then dumped him by the roadside. The torture was brutal and he had to be hospitalised for weeks. He suffered multiple fractures in his legs, a severe burn on his foot, internal injuries in his abdomen and cuts and bruises on his head.[11] The men used a piece of wood to crush the fingers on his right hand to 'stop [him] from writing' – they also shaved his head and beard, then pushed the hair into his mouth to muffle his screams.[12]

In interviews with human rights groups and US diplomats, Jayantha held three senior leaders of the national security establishment responsible for his ordeal: Lieutenant Colonel Gotabaya Rajapaksa, General Sarath Fonseka and IGP Jayantha Wickramaratne. In the past, Rajapaksa had admonished him in private for his press freedom advocacy and journalism while Fonseka and Wickramaratne publicly labelled journalists and press freedom advocates like him as 'traitors funded by the LTTE'. In December 2009, Jayantha left Sri Lanka with his family (wife and a daughter) and went into exile in the United States.

Persecution of intellectuals – one of the key features of the national security state – had been a routine affair in Sri Lanka for decades. It first began as part of a security crackdown against the Janatha Vimukthi Peramuna (JVP, People's Liberation Front), a revolutionary communist party. During this crackdown journalists, writers and artists were targeted by the security forces for their ties with the JVP. Hundreds of them were imprisoned and tortured – some were murdered. One of the most infamous cases of murder was the abduction and execution of Richard de Zoysa – a journalist, human rights activist and actor.

de Zoysa was a correspondent for the Inter Press Service. He was also a rising star of Colombo's cultural scene. He was abducted by an unidentified group of armed men who broke into his home in the early morning on 18 February 1990. His body – with a fractured jaw, burn marks, and bullet holes in the head and throat – was dumped near a beach on the following day. His mother held a police death squad responsible for his murder.[13]

The brutal and sinister murder of Richard de Zoysa led to a protest movement against extrajudicial executions and enforced disappearances. His mother Manorani Saravanamuttu founded the Mother's Front in July 1990, demanding justice for the victims of abuses perpetrated by police death squads.[14] One of the co-founders of the front was Mahinda Rajapaksa, then a junior MP of the opposition Sri Lanka Freedom Party (SLFP). He was a fearless advocate defending the victims of state terror and their families. After narrowly winning the presidential election of 2005, he took over as the new president of Sri Lanka and then became the chief political sponsor of its white van death squads.[15]

The Rajapaksa government was ruthless against its opponents, especially journalists who were critical of the president, his brother Gotabaya Rajapaksa and their cronies. These critical journalists were targeted for systematic persecution by the security forces and other government agencies – censorship, imprisonment, torture, murder and enforced disappearance were the abuses meted out to the press. Also, some ministers and senior government officials publicly threatened individual journalists. Following these attacks and threats, more than 30 journalists fled the country and had gone into exile since 2006. The abuses continued even after the end of the civil war, as the Rajapaksa brothers consolidated their power in post-war Sri Lanka.[16]

One of the critics of the government and the security forces was the journalist and cartoonist Prageeth Eknaligoda. As a correspondent for the news website Lanka E-news, he was investigating allegations regarding the use of chemical weapons by the army against the LTTE rebels. He also briefed Western diplomats in Colombo about the investigation and its findings. Sri Lanka had been a party to the Chemical Weapons Convention since 1997 and the government always denied allegations about the use of chemical weapons during the civil war.

In August 2009, Eknaligoda was abducted by a white van death squad who released him after some hours. Then in January 2010, he disappeared from the streets of Colombo, forever. Eyewitnesses later described the presence of a white van in the area where he was last seen. His wife, Sandhya Eknaligoda, pointed to his investigation into chemical weapons as the main reason for his abduction and enforced disappearance.[17]

Since Rajapaksa became the president in 2005, enforced disappearance by men in white vans had been a recurrent nightmare for thousands of Sri Lankans. In a report published in 2008, Human Rights Watch (HRW) presented the results of its investigation into 99 enforced disappearances which took place between December 2005 and June 2007 – in at least 27 of these cases, the victims had been driven away in white vans by their captors.[18] Meanwhile, Sri Lankan human rights groups documented 498 enforced disappearances which took place between March 2006 and January 2007.[19] The WGEID (Working Group on Enforced or Involuntary Disappearances, a human rights monitoring body of the United Nations) documented 573 cases between November 2005 and September 2014 – at least 101 enforced disappearances reported to the WGEID took place after the end of the civil war. The WGEID had been documenting cases of enforced disappearances in Sri Lanka for decades. From 1980 to 2013, it recorded a total of 12,473 cases – in 6,445 of these cases, the victims were later reported dead.[20]

The exact numbers of disappearances and deaths, however, would be much higher. According to investigations carried out by four Sri Lankan commissions of inquiry and the National Human Rights Commission, there were at least 21,600 cases of enforced disappearances between January 1988 and December 1994.[21] Most of these cases were connected to the civil war and the security crackdown on the JVP – in only a small number of these cases (less than 500), the perpetrators were prosecuted. These enforced disappearances were part of the larger military campaign and security crackdown during which brutal acts of violence were perpetrated by all sides – the security forces, the LTTE and the JVP.

Since 1983, the security forces had perpetrated war crimes and crimes against humanity in northern and eastern Sri Lanka: the massacre of Tamil civilians; the indiscriminate bombing of civilian areas; attacks on medical facilities and places of worship; the forced displacement of civilians; and torture and extrajudicial execution.[22] The LTTE was also responsible for war crimes, crimes against humanity and human rights abuses: the killing of civilians; the recruitment of child soldiers; suicide bombing against civilian targets; the massacre and ethnic cleansing of Sinhalese and Muslims; the assassination of political opponents, journalists and activists; and torture and extrajudicial execution.[23] As the JVP waged an armed insurgency against the government between 1987 and 1990, militant JVP activists engaged in acts of terrorism and violence: assassinations, bomb attacks and violent street riots. In response, police death squads carried out extrajudicial executions of suspected JVP members. These murders were gruesome and the mutilated bodies of the victims were often displayed in public.[24]

The LTTE rebels and the JVP militants did not have the massive financial and organisational capacity of the state to bolster their campaigns of violence and repression – nor were they backed by black laws. The Sri Lankan security forces were hailed as heroes for re-establishing or enforcing the state's monopoly on violence by perpetrating crimes in a proclaimed state of emergency. The LTTE and the JVP were described as terrorist groups for perpetrating the same or similar crimes as part of their armed rebellion against the state. This was the primary difference between state terror and terrorism – between saviours and terrorists.

Sri Lanka spent LKR1.249 trillion to cover the war effort between 1988 and 2009.[25] LKR175 billion (US$1.5 billion) was spent in 2009, the final year of the civil war – this was 3.6 per cent of GDP and 17.3 per cent of central government expenditure.[26] The money was spent in military procurement and to sustain an expansive network of armed forces, paramilitary forces, national security agencies, defence colleges and branches of the ministry of defence. These were the institutions of the national security state.

The national security laws of Sri Lanka deprived the citizens of their fundamental human rights and empowered the security forces to engage in systematic campaigns of state terror. These black laws were designed to terrorise the population and shield agents of the state from censure or prosecution for abuses. Some of these laws were de facto licences for torture, murder and enforced disappearance.

The foundation of Sri Lanka's black laws and its state of emergency was the Public Security Ordinance of 1947 – a piece of law enacted by the British rulers of Ceylon (now Sri Lanka). The law was designed by the colonial administration to suppress political dissent and opposition. In independent Sri Lanka, ostensibly democratic presidents used the ordinance to declare states of emergency, to enact emergency regulations and to deploy the military 'in the interests' of public security and public order. The ordinance was repeatedly invoked during the war against the LTTE and in the crackdown against the JVP, especially to grant police powers to the members of the armed forces. It was also the basis for a series of emergency laws or regulations which suspended the constitutional rights of the citizens and indemnified the security forces.[27]

The Prevention of Terrorism (Temporary Provisions) Act of 1979 was used by the police against suspected members of the LTTE and the JVP. It was a de facto licence for the secret detention (enforced disappearance) of a 'proclaimed person' (suspected terrorist). The act empowered the police to arrest any person without a warrant and hold the suspect in preventive detention without charge or trial for up to 18 months – the police were empowered to take a 'proclaimed person' to 'any place for the purpose of interrogation' and move the detainee 'from place to place for the purposes of investigation.'[28] The act also granted police officers warrantless search and seizure powers. Article 23 of the act provided the officers with blanket immunity from civil or criminal prosecution.

One of the key features of the Sri Lankan war effort was the proliferation of emergency laws. The government used a provision in the Public Security Ordinance to enact 'emergency regulations', bypassing constitutional legislation processes. These regulations superseded 'any [other] law' of the land. The latest of these were the Emergency (Miscellaneous Provisions and Powers) Regulations of 2005 and the Emergency (Prevention and Prohibition of Terrorism and Specified Terrorist Activities) Regulations of 2006.

The emergency regulations of 2005 granted the government extraordinary powers in relation to people suspected of 'acting in any manner prejudicial to national security.' The secretary of defence could order preventive/administrative detention of these people for up to 18 months, without any judicial scrutiny. The detainees could be held incommunicado in secret, unofficial holding facilities as per the instructions from the secretary of defence or the inspector general of the police – in case of a detainee's death, the deputy inspector general of the police was authorised to secretly dispose of the body (bury or cremate) 'in the interest of national security or for the maintenance or preservation of public order.'[29] The regulations also granted broad police powers to the armed forces: arrest, detention, search and seizure without a warrant. Regulation 73 of the regulations of 2005 provided government officials and the security forces with blanket immunity from prosecution for abuses.

The emergency regulations of 2006 provided broad and vague definitions of 'terrorism', 'terrorist activity' and 'acts of terrorism' which enabled the security forces to use the Prevention of Terrorism

(Temporary Provisions) Act and other anti-terrorism laws against suspected LTTE members and sympathisers. These definitions were designed to extend the original scope of the act of 1979. The regulations also renewed and strengthened the immunity provision for government officials and the security forces by stipulating:

No action or suit shall lie against any public servant or any other person specifically authorized by the government of Sri Lanka to take action in terms of these regulations, provided that such person has acted in good faith and in the discharge of his official duties.[30]

The LTTE was proscribed as a terrorist group not only in Sri Lanka but also in many other countries across the globe. The group was notorious worldwide for inventing the suicide belt and perfecting the technique of suicide bombing. It also pioneered the use of women in suicide attacks and assassinated two world leaders – Rajiv Gandhi (former prime minister of India) and Ranasinghe Premadasa (president of Sri Lanka).[31] In the international system, Sri Lanka's sovereign right to destroy this death cult was widely recognised.

Notable among the countries that declared the LTTE to be a terrorist organisation were India, the United States, the United Kingdom, Canada and members of the European Union. However, these countries mostly refrained from delivering military aid or selling weapons to Sri Lanka due to domestic politics and allegations of war crimes and human rights abuses. Some of these countries wanted to have a political settlement of the conflict instead of a military solution. China, Israel and Pakistan, on the other hand, emerged as major economic and military backers of the Sri Lankan war effort.[32] After the war, China also became the main international sponsor of the Rajapaksa government, especially at the United Nations.

China had been the largest supplier of conventional weapons to Sri Lanka since 1950. Arms transfer from China to Sri Lanka significantly increased during the civil war. A small share of this transfer was provided as military aid. In 1991, the two countries signed an arms deal worth US$104 million. In 1993, a major Chinese arms producer and exporter, NORINCO, set up a bonded warehouse near the south-western city of Galle to ensure the rapid supply of weapons to the Sri Lankan forces. In 2007, another major Chinese arms producer and exporter, Poly Technologies, started offering similar services. Between 2005 and 2010, Sri Lanka became the eighth largest market for Chinese weapons: small arms, light weapons, ammunition, landmines, naval vessels and combat aircraft.[33]

China was not only the biggest seller of weapons but also a staunch proponent of Sri Lanka's right to buy weapons. As a Chinese policymaker commented during an interview:

We have to understand that the Sri Lankan conflict lasted for three decades and that thousands died. The LTTE were terrorists, as even the [United Nations] agreed. The Sri Lankan government was a legitimate sovereign state actor to procure arms. The end of the war was good news and we need to be frank that it was not mediation that achieved it.[34]

This position was in line with one of the key features of Chinese foreign policy – the relentless championing of state sovereignty even at the expense of human rights. To some degree, it was also influenced by China's economic and strategic interests in the Indian Ocean and its own trouble with separatism in Tibet and Xinjiang.[35]

At the international level, China's political patronage of the Sri Lankan government was most visible at the United Nations. In March 2009, as the Sri Lankan forces escalated their attacks against LTTE positions, China blocked all discussions about the conflict at the Security Council of the United Nations.[36] This, in effect, barred the international community from taking any concrete action regarding the rising number of civilian deaths in northern Sri Lanka – it also gave the Sri Lankan government a free rein to defeat the LTTE.

In May 2009, China helped Sri Lanka in blocking an international investigation into allegations of war crimes and crimes against humanity during the final stages of the civil war. This was at the Human Rights Council of the United Nations, where some European states tried to pass a resolution in favour of an investigation. China led 29 other member states of the council in passing another resolution that blocked any such investigation. The resolution, authored by Sri Lankan delegates, congratulated the Sri Lankan government for liberating northern Sri Lanka by defeating the LTTE and reaffirmed 'the principle of non-interference in matters which [were] essentially within the domestic jurisdiction of states.'[37]

In June 2010, when Ban Ki-moon, the Secretary General of the United Nations, established a panel of experts to investigate allegations of war crimes and crimes against humanity during the final stages of the war, China opposed the move by citing the Sri Lankan government's own investigation as credible and sufficient.[38] In April 2011, the panel of experts published a report noting evidence of war crimes and crimes against humanity perpetrated by the Sri Lankan forces and the LTTE. Once again, Chinese diplomats opposed any international action regarding these allegations, saying that these were Sri Lanka's internal matters.[39]

In June 2011, the Chinese delegation at the Human Rights Council opposed the creation of an 'international monitoring mechanism' on Sri Lanka. As the Chinese foreign minister assured his Sri Lankan counterpart during a meeting, '[China had] total confidence in the capability of the government and people of Sri Lanka to resolve their own issues.'[40]

In September 2011, one of the most powerful Chinese politicians, Wu Bangguo, assured the Sri Lankan Prime Minister Disanayaka Jayaratne of continual support, '[China would] continue to support Sri Lanka's efforts to safeguard its national independence, sovereignty and territorial integrity as well as respect Sri Lanka's path of development and its domestic and foreign policies.'[41] China had been keeping this promise by bankrolling large-scale development and infrastructure projects in post-war Sri Lanka – between 2009 and 2014, Sri Lanka received US\$4 billion from China in loans, grants and economic aid.[42]

In many ways, there were remarkable similarities between China's political and military sponsorship of Sri Lanka and the United States' relentless sponsorship of Israel. In order to protect Sri Lanka and aid its war effort, China used the same tactics that had been used by the United States to protect Israel and aid its occupation of Palestine – engineering deadlocks at the United Nations Security Council and blocking international investigations into allegations of war crimes and crimes against humanity. Also, in both cases, the rival superpowers transferred massive amounts of weapons to their respective client states, citing the need to destroy terrorist groups like the LTTE and Hamas. All of these were at the expense of civilian populations – Tamils during the Sri Lankan siege of Vanni and Palestinians during the Israeli siege of Gaza.

Israel had been one of the major military sponsors of Sri Lanka since the onset of the war. Israel's arms transfer, however, started even before that, when it sold two frigates to Sri Lanka in 1959. In 1984, the military ties were renewed as Sri Lanka was looking for international advisers for its counter-insurgency operations. Israel was the only country that responded positively to Sri Lanka's request for assistance. In a deal chaperoned by the United States, it sent six Shabak (Israel's internal security agency) officers to Sri Lanka to train the Sri Lankan army in counter-insurgency techniques. This programme was coordinated by Mossad (Israel's national intelligence agency). The Israeli security advisers helped the Sri Lankan government to design its national security network and create a counter-insurgency unit – the Special Task Force (STF). In other words, Israeli experts midwifed the birth of the Sri Lankan national security state. According to some reports, they were also the masterminds behind a Sinhalese settlement building programme in Tamil areas.[43]

Since 1996, Sri Lanka had relied heavily on Israel to arm its air force and navy. Israel primarily had exported warships, naval vessels and combat aircraft to Sri Lanka. For the Sri Lankan Navy, Israeli warships and Dvora class patrol boats had been crucial in defeating the LTTE in sea battles. The Sri Lanka Air Force, meanwhile, acquired Kfir fighter jets from Israel to upgrade its fleet. In 2001, the air force also deployed four Israeli Scout and Searcher drones (UAV) in the battlefield. In 2007, seven Scout and Blue Horizon drones were added to the fleet. Sri Lankan procurement of Israeli patrol boats continued even after the end of the war.[44]

Apart from China and Israel, Sri Lanka had also relied on unquestioned support and supply of weapons from Pakistan – its staunchest ally in South Asia. In 1985, Pakistan was one of the few countries that delivered military aid to Sri Lanka. In 2000, it delivered an emergency assistance package of rocket launchers in response to an appeal by the Sri Lankan government. Since then, Sri Lanka relied on a steady supply of ammunition from Pakistan – mortar shells, grenades and bullets. Sri Lanka had used a yearly line of credit – US$80 million – to pay for the supplies.[45] And like China, Pakistan's ties with Sri Lanka had been influenced by its own history of ethnic conflicts and separatism, especially in Balochistan.

Pakistan also provided the Sri Lankan generals with a model for sustaining the national security state through the creation of an expansive military economy. After the end of the war in 2009, the Sri Lankan military embarked on hundreds of business ventures – shopping malls, hotels, resorts, restaurants, veterinary clinics, cruise ships, security companies and travel agencies.[46] All of these were based on a business model copied from Pakistan which would allow serving and retired members of the armed forces to become powerful players in the national economy. This was the birth of Sri Lanka's own 'Military Inc' or Milbus.

The history of the Sri Lankan civil war is also the history of a post-colonial state transforming into an archetypal national security state. It is a transformation that was engendered by the Sri Lankan ruling elite who used a piece of colonial black law (the Public Security Ordinance of 1947) to impose a permanent state of emergency in the island nation. This state of emergency was the cradle for the specialists on violence who emerged as the ultimate saviours of the motherland. These were saviours who were celebrated as national heroes by the government, media and general public who lauded their crimes as 'the real way to fight terrorism'. It was against this backdrop of the jingoistic veneration of the military, that Sri Lanka's white vans first started roaming the streets of Colombo and Jaffna. These vans were not only the vehicles of state terror but also the symbols of the absolute militarisation of the society. It is a society that has been engaged in a brutal war with itself for more than two decades – a dirty war against internal enemies, that went on even after the defeat of the LTTE.

7

STATE TERROR IN POST-COLONIAL SOUTH ASIA

The four colonial siblings of South Asia – Bangladesh, India, Pakistan and Sri Lanka – are the progeny of the British Raj.[1] Designed and enforced by colonial specialists on violence, the Raj was an elaborate system of administering control and domination – a system that these post-colonial states inherited with their independence between 1947 and 1971. The history of independence in South Asia is the history of amendments and revisions to the original colonial order. It is a history of how the ruling elite in the post-colonial state tried to perfect the organs of state terror which were originally designed by their colonial predecessors. *Amendment*, indeed, is one of the most favourite words of South Asian lawmakers in Colombo, Delhi, Dhaka and Islamabad, especially when they revise the black laws of the colonial administration and recycle them to sponsor new campaigns of terror and violence against internal enemies.

On the other hand, the history of Nepal (the only country in the region which was never a part of the Raj) is the history of a British tributary or vassal state.[2] The monarchy that had been ruling the Himalayan nation was the product of a series of arrangements between Nepalese kings (Shah dynasty), hereditary prime ministers (Rana dynasty) and the British rulers of India. These arrangements allowed the monarchy to maintain nominal independence while supplying the Raj with a steady flow of mercenary foot soldiers.[3] Indeed, Gurkha soldiers recruited from Nepal were an integral part of the colonial British Indian Army – some Gurkha soldiers were involved in the Jallianwala Bagh Massacre of 1919.[4] To this day, special Gurkha regiments remain attached to British and Indian military forces. After the end of the Raj, Nepalese soldiers became the principal saviours or sentinels of the Nepalese monarchy. Nepal became a democratic republic only in 2008, after the overthrow of the monarchy in 2006. For the people of Nepal, independence (in the form of democracy) came only after the overthrow of the system of repression originally imposed or aided by the British colonial order. In other words, South Asia is invariably shaped by the legacies of British colonialism.

The history of state terror in South Asia correlates with the region's post-colonial geography. The emergence of new metropolises and the creation of new colonies are the two key features of this geography. The new rulers of South Asia not only improved the colonial machinery of state terror by deploying innovative tools like the death squad but also adopted the mechanisms of colonial plunder of the periphery. The Raj, of course, was also an elaborate system of economic exploitation of the subcontinent. It was a system of massive transfer of wealth and resources from the colony to the mother country – to the metropolis of London. After the end of the Raj, new and shiny metropolises now dot the subcontinent. And these metropolises, which store and showcase the wealth of a new generation of millionaires and billionaires, are also surrounded by areas marred by chronic poverty. This is recurrent in every country and every major city of the region where an opulently rich core is surrounded by an impoverished and often restive periphery.

Pervasive structural violence (socio-political injustices) in the peripheries of the world capitalist system is a feature of the new economic order in our post-colonial world.[5] The new peripheries of South Asia are restive not only because of the structural violence resultant from economic exploitation but also because of the coercive governance (ruling without consent of the governed) by post-colonial states.[6] This problem of coercive governance is latent even in ostensibly democratic polities across the region. Structural violence and coercive governance are the main issues behind the three major challenges facing the post-colonial state: the emergence of a class of dissident intellectuals and activists who challenge the hegemony of the state and its ruling elite; the outbreak of new insurgencies (based on class, ethnicity or religion) in the periphery that threaten the state's monopoly on violence; and the formation of a criminal underworld that threatens the socio-economic security and stability of the new metropolis.

The post-colonial state responds to the challenges of criticism/ activism, insurgency and organised crime by unleashing its specialists on violence against its internal enemies – the dissident intellectuals/activists, the rebels/insurgents of the periphery and the lumpenproletariat of the metropolis. In South Asia, silencing of dissent and establishing the government's monopoly on violence are the principal goals of governance. Reliance on the ever-expansive capacity of violence by the police, paramilitary and military forces is the key administrative principle of the ruling elite.[7] Across the subcontinent, this militarism of the ruling elite proliferates in the form of black laws, which are used to rob the citizens of their rights and to deploy death squads as saviours, sentinels and custodians of the national security state.[8]

In post colonial South Asia, the saviours first appeared with the partition of India in 1947. The partition divided the British Indian empire into two new countries: India and Pakistan. In the process, it also transformed India – the erstwhile colony – into a new mother country (*Bharat Mata*, Mother India) surrounded by new colonies. During the first few years of independence, the central government of India set out to recolonise the north-eastern states and the northern state of Jammu and Kashmir. These peripheral states were brought under Indian rule through the systematic use of violence and coercion. In these states, campaigns of terror are still ongoing. Even then, a significant number of Assamese, Kashmiris, Manipuris, Mizos, Nagas and Tripuris remain opposed to India's rule of their homelands.[9] In only one case, in the north-western state of Punjab, has the government been successful in quelling separatism, after waging brutal counter-insurgency operations for more than a decade. India, indeed, has been waging internal wars against separatist rebels and insurgents since its birth.

In the states along the Red Corridor, India has had to deal with another crisis which has resulted from the endemic structural violence against the *adivasi*s and the landless peasants. These subalterns are now being mobilised by the Communist Party of India (Maoist) as part of a 'people's war' – a war of the periphery against the centre; a war between Maoist *adivasi*s and Indian paramilitary forces. In many ways, it is also a war of the dispossessed against the forces of economic globalisation – Indian and global conglomerates who are keen on exploiting natural resources buried under indigenous lands.[10] In order to protect corporate interests and to silence dissenting voices, the Indian government has also embarked on a campaign of judicial persecution against troublesome intellectuals like Binayak Sen and G.N. Saibaba – activists and academics advocating for *adivasi* rights.[11] Since the government of Prime Minister Narendra Modi came to power in 2014, there has also been a crackdown against activist groups like Greenpeace India and Amnesty International, which are labelled as 'anti-national' and 'anti-development' troublemakers funded by foreign donors.[12]

In other parts of India, structural violence and socio-economic injustices have forced millions of Indians to become internal migrants. These migrants flow into the new metropolises in search of economic security and become residents of the biggest slums in Asia.[13] This massive flow of migration from the villages to the slums is the main cause of the rise of a new class of lumpenproletariat in the metropolis. The metropolis is not only home to India's ruling elite and its billionaires but is also the breeding ground for organised crime syndicates and gangs (like the dreaded Indian Mafia), invariably led by lumpenproletariat migrants like Manya Surve and Dawood Ibrahim Kaskar.[14] Indeed, some of the earliest cases of encounter killings and deployment of encounter specialists in India were linked to the police crackdown on Mumbai's criminal underworld – a crackdown aimed at 'cleaning the city' (to quote Pradeep Sharma of the Mumbai encounter squad) by executing socio-economic troublemakers.

Extrajudicial execution in the form of encounter killings in the peripheries and the metropolises is a relatively recent feature of state terror in India. However, post-colonial India's machinery of terror is nothing more than a revised and updated version of the machinery of colonial violence and control designed by the British Raj. The government of India not only uses colonial paramilitary forces like the Assam Rifles and the Central Reserve Police Force (erstwhile Crown Representative's Police) to subjugate the people of the periphery but it also sponsors their campaigns of terror through black laws modelled after the draconian Rowlatt Act of 1919. India's national security laws are not only 'restrictive of human liberty' (to quote Mohandas Gandhi) but are also de facto licences for abuse by the security forces. These laws, in effect, impose a permanent state of exception (state of emergency) in disturbed or troubled areas where the police and paramilitary forces perpetrate abuse with absolute impunity. In promulgating black laws, ostensibly democratic lawmakers in Delhi have outdone their colonial predecessors in the Imperial Legislative Council of London.[15]

The proliferation of black laws is one of the key features of statecraft in South Asia, as lawmakers across the region rely on national security legislation to sponsor state terror campaigns. National security laws are legal instruments that set apart the agents of state terror from the enemies of the state, and state crimes from crimes against the state. These laws fall into two broad categories: legal devices for restricting human liberty and legal devices for militarising law and order. In both categories, members of the security forces and government officials are granted immunity from prosecution for abuses codifying such immunity into the law is of course vital for the deployment of death squads across South Asia.[16]

Black laws in the first category – devices for restricting human liberty – are revised and updated with more stringent versions of the Rowlatt Act of 1919 that rob the citizens of their fundamental rights and grant extraordinary powers to the agents of the state in the name of national security, public order and counter-terrorism.[17] These laws include the Special Powers Act of 1974 (Bangladesh), the National Security Act of 1980 (India), the Public Security Act of 1989/1991 (Nepal) and the Anti-Terrorism Act of 1997 (Pakistan). Two laws in Sri Lanka, enacted during the civil war, are especially representative of this category of black laws: the Prevention of Terrorism (Temporary Provisions) Act of 1979 and the Emergency (Miscellaneous Provisions and Powers) Regulations of 2005.

The Prevention of Terrorism (Temporary Provisions) Act of 1979 allows the Sri Lankan police to arrest any 'proclaimed person' without a warrant and hold that person in secret/unofficial detention facilities without charge or trial for up to 18 months. The Emergency (Miscellaneous Provisions and Powers) Regulations of 2005 (no longer in force) granted extraordinary powers to the government for dealing with a person who acted 'in any manner prejudicial to national security'. Such a person could be held incommunicado in secret/unofficial detention facilities for up to 18 months without any judicial supervision. The regulations also carried a specific provision for the secret burial or cremation of a detainee's body (in case of death in custody). Both the act and the regulations provided agents of the state (government officials and security forces) immunity from civil or criminal prosecution for abuses. During the Sri Lankan civil war, these two laws were used by the Sri Lankan police and other security forces as de facto licences for enforced disappearance.

In the second category, two black laws in Bangladesh and India are representative examples of legal devices used for militarising law and order: the Armed Police Battalions Ordinance of 1979/2003 (Bangladesh), which incorporates many of the provisions of the Army Act of 1952 (a Pakistan era law); and the Armed Forces (Special Powers) Act of 1958 (India), which is a revised version of the Armed Forces (Special Powers) Ordinance of 1942, promulgated by the Raj for suppressing Mohandas Gandhi's 'Quit India' movement. These two laws grant extraordinary police powers to members of the armed forces and enable their deployment as part of paramilitary death squads like the Rapid Action Battalion (Bangladesh), the Assam Rifles (India) or the Rashtriya Rifles (India). The Bangladeshi ordinance of 1979/2003 and the Indian act of 1958 shield the commanders and personnel of these paramilitary death squads from prosecution or censure for abuses.

Elsewhere in South Asia, such laws include the Terrorist and Disruptive (Control and Punishment) Act of 2002 (Nepal), the Protection of Pakistan Act of 2014 and the Public Security Ordinance of 1947 (Sri Lanka) – in Nepal, the act of 2002 was used to authorise terror campaigns by the Royal Nepalese Army, during the civil war; in Pakistan, the act of 2014 is used to authorise the deployment of military and paramilitary troops in counter-insurgency operations or internal wars against Baloch nationalists and TTP insurgents; in Sri Lanka, the ordinance of 1947 was used to deploy the Sri Lankan armed forces in the war against the LTTE.

The three functions of black laws – suspending fundamental rights, deploying military/paramilitary troops and indemnifying agents of the state – correlate with the functions of a state of emergency and martial law. A state of emergency is a constitutional mechanism through which the government creates a state of exception in times of national crisis, by suspending parts of the constitution and granting itself extraordinary and coercive powers. This, by definition, is a temporary and exceptional form of governance which deviates from the regular and democratic constitutional order. Martial law, on the other hand, is the coercive suspension of the constitutional order by the military and its commanders. This, too, is an exceptional form of governance which aims to militarise all the branches and functions of the government. In South Asia, black laws are designed to impose an extended and permanent state of exception by suspending the fundamental rights of the citizens even when the constitution is not suspended and militarising law and order even when martial law is not in force.[18] The Armed Forces (Special Powers) Act of India and the Protection of Pakistan Act are archetypal black laws used to create permanent states of exception, especially in the peripheries.

The history of state terror in South Asia correlates with the history of state of emergency and martial law in the region. In Bangladesh, the first state of emergency was declared in 1974, followed by the first martial law proclamation in 1975 – these were followed by another martial law proclamation in 1982 and two more state of emergency declarations in 1987 and 2007.[19] In India, a state of emergency was declared during the Sino-Indian war of 1962 and the Indo-Pakistani war of 1971 – between 1975 and 1977, another state of emergency was imposed by the government of Indira Gandhi, ostensibly to deal with 'internal disturbance'.[20] In Nepal, a state of emergency was declared by its kings three times: in 1960, 2001 and 2005.[21] Pakistani military dictators imposed martial law in their country three times: in 1958, 1969 and 1977.[22] General Pervez Musharraf, on the other hand, imposed a state of emergency twice: in 1999 and 2007.[23] In Sri Lanka, successive governments have imposed a state of emergency since 1971 – the island was under an unbroken state of emergency between 2005 and 2011.[24]

Indeed, new paradigms of post-colonial terror were first developed by South Asian governments against the backdrop of a state of emergency (Bangladesh, India, Nepal and Sri Lanka) and martial law (Bangladesh and Pakistan). Across the subcontinent, declarations of a state of emergency and proclamations of martial law were invariably used as instruments to quell disorder and disobedience. These were the times when the national security state emerged in full view – no longer hidden behind the façade of democracy and rule of law.

In Pakistan, the birth of the national security state was facilitated by the imposition of martial law in October 1958. This was proclaimed by Major General (retired) Iskander Mirza, the first president of Pakistan, in response to a constitutional crisis in which the Pakistani military engineered consecutive removals and resignations of four civilian prime ministers between 1955 and 1957.[25] A few days after the imposition of martial law, Mirza himself was disposed in a bloodless coup led by Ayub Khan – the chief martial law administrator and the commander-in-chief of the army. Khan appointed himself as the new president of Pakistan and set out to transform the newly independent country into an archetypal garrison state.[26]

As the new military dictator of Pakistan, Ayub Khan faced his first major challenge in Balochistan where Baloch nationalist parties started opposing his regime through an armed rebellion. In response, between 1958 and 1969, the Pakistan Army launched a series of counter-insurgency operations targeting Baloch leaders, activists and rebels. These operations and the establishment of new military bases across the province transformed Balochistan into one of the most militarised regions of the country.[27] The second major challenge for Ayub Khan was from the Bengali nationalists of East Pakistan. Here, the new president activated the MI (Military Intelligence), the IB (Intelligence Bureau) and the ISI (Inter-Services Intelligence) against the leaders and activists of the Awami League. These intelligence agencies were tasked with carrying out covert operations (dirty ops) against Bengali politicians and intellectuals – this was the first time Pakistan's security agencies (especially the ISI) were used in a concerted campaign against internal enemies.[28] In other words, the martial law of 1958 was the beginning of Pakistan's dirty wars led by its army and security agencies.

Since then, abrogating the constitution and imposing martial law or a state of emergency has become the standard operating procedure for Pakistan's military whenever it has faced major trouble or crisis. Ayub Khan's successor, General Yahya Khan, imposed martial law in 1969, responding to the political crisis in East Pakistan.[29] In 1977, General Zia-ul-Haq imposed another martial law to overthrow the elected government of Zulfikar Ali Bhutto, following a political crisis.[30] In 1999, General Pervez Musharraf declared a state of emergency as he overthrew the elected government of Nawaz Sharif in a bloodless coup, following the fourth Indo-Pakistani war (Kargil war).[31] In 2007, Musharraf once again declared a state of emergency as the legality of his presidency was being tested by the Supreme Court of Pakistan.[32] All of these invariably marked the beginning of new dirty wars waged by the military against Pakistan's internal enemies.[33]

Across South Asia, declarations of a state of emergency or martial law always signalled the beginning of state terror campaigns in which death squads would be deployed against internal enemies. In Pakistan, the martial law of 1969 led to the creation of al Badr in 1971, as part of the counter-insurgency operations in East Pakistan. Then, after the secession of East Pakistan, the martial law of 1977 enabled the rise of the ISI as the principal organ of state terror in the country. In Bangladesh, the state of emergency in 1974 was used to deploy the Jatiyo Rakkhi Bahini in a brutal crackdown against opposition parties, dissident intellectuals, *sarbahara* groups and internal migrants displaced by the famine.[34] This was followed by martial law regimes imposed between 1975 and 1990, which enabled the rise of the DGFI as the principal national security agency of the country, responsible for dirty ops against opposition parties and political dissidents. In India, the state of emergency in 1975 was used by the government of Indira Gandhi for a brutal police crackdown against opposition parties and political dissidents. In Sri Lanka, the state of emergency in 2005 led to the creation and deployment of white van death squads. In Nepal, Royal Nepalese Army death squads first emerged against the backdrop of a state of emergency in 2001.

A state of emergency and martial law, in other words, have always been the cradle of South Asian death squads. While these death squads were mostly post-colonial innovations, the use of a state of emergency and martial law as mechanisms for creating a state of exception have had their roots in the British colonial era. Indeed, these paradigms of repression were first developed by the government of George V in response to the outbreak of the First World War in 1914 – after the end of the war, the emergency powers of the monarch were codified in the Emergency Powers Act of 1920.[35] In British India, emergency powers for the administrators of the Raj and martial law powers for commanders of the British Indian Army were first codified in the Defence of India Act of 1915, the Government of India Act of 1915 and the Rowlatt Act of 1919.[36] In incorporating emergency provisions into the constitutions of India, Pakistan, Sri Lanka and Bangladesh, post-colonial jurists in these countries were indeed guided by these three laws of the Raj – laws that introduced the model for dealing with crisis, trouble and rebellion through the suspension of fundamental rights and the deployment of the army and other security forces against internal enemies.[37]

For millions of people in South Asia's peripheries, the post-colonial state is nothing more than a system of repression and exploitation, imposed and administered by an undemocratic ruling elite. It is a system in which terror is the most consistently employed tool of governance. Across the subcontinent, this system is sustained through the widespread proliferation of black laws. These are the laws that transform enemies of the state into *homo sacers* who are abducted, tortured and executed by South Asian death squads – *jallads* protected through the state of exception created by the state. In a practical sense, these laws are the real constitution of new colonies and disturbed areas. Black laws, in other words, are the first pillar of the system of state terror in post-colonial South Asia.

8

SPECIALISTS ON VIOLENCE

Every year, India celebrates Republic Day on 26 January, marking the anniversary of the Indian constitution. The constitution was adopted in 1950, replacing the colonial Government of India Act of 1935. It was the founding document through which the new rulers of India promised its citizens justice ('social, economic and political'), liberty ('of thought, expression, belief, faith and worship') and equality ('of status and of opportunity') in an independent country, free from the shackles of colonial exploitation and repression. As many Indians often boast on Republic Day, this constitution (the longest in the world, with 448 articles) is a living document that governs the affairs of the largest democracy in the world. Some Indians, however, also question why the annual Republic Day celebrations in Delhi are focused on India's military might instead of its constitutional promises and democratic achievements.[1] India's Republic Day, in effect, is not a celebration of democracy, constitutional order or rule of law – rather, it is one of the most important public rituals of the Indian national security state.[2] It is an annual event that confirms the priority of the Indian state, that is sustaining one of the largest militaries in the world instead of ensuring fundamental rights of the citizens.[3]

In Delhi, Republic Day begins with the prime minister placing a floral wreath in front of Amar Jawan Jyoti (flame of the immortal soldier), a monument commemorating martyred Indian soldiers. The monument (built in 1972) is located under the arch of the famous India Gate (built in 1917), itself a war memorial, commemorating British-Indian soldiers who died during the First World War.[4] This is a monument that immortalises the indomitable Indian soldier, who once served the British Raj and who is now serving the Indian republic. And every year, the prime minister of the republic returns to this monument to pay homage to the soldier through an elaborately choreographed ceremony that involves a guard of honour, a salute with arms and bugle playing.[5]

The ritual veneration of the dead soldier is followed by the main Republic Day event that takes place in the form of a jingoistic military parade – with columns of soldiers marching and rows of tanks rolling through the streets of the capital.[6] Among the paramilitary forces that take part in the two-hour-long parade are the Assam Rifles, the Rashtriya Rifles and the Central Reserve Police Force – paramilitary death squads responsible for protecting 'the unity and integrity of the nation' (as enshrined in the constitution) through abduction, torture and extrajudicial execution. These forces are the real saviours of Mother India and the real custodians of the ostensible republic, venerated and celebrated as national heroes by the government, the media and the general public. Like many other countries across the globe, tanks, missile launchers and combat aircraft on display during the Republic Day parade are the real symbols of the post-colonial order in India.

Similar national rituals that involve military parades and the worshipping of dead soldiers like martyred patron saints are also observed by other governments in the region, albeit on different dates and in different forms: in Bangladesh, the president and the prime minister begin Armed Forces Day on 21 November by placing floral wreaths in front of Shikha Anirban (eternal flame), a monument located inside the Dhaka cantonment (headquarters of the army, navy and air force); in Sri Lanka, Independence Day is celebrated on 4 February with a grand military parade in Colombo; in Pakistan, Republic Day (Pakistan Day) is celebrated on 23 March with a grand military parade in Islamabad.[7] These rituals are symptomatic of the national security state, where *independence* and *democracy* are mere euphemisms of militarism; where the constitutional power of the government often translates into a licence for state terror.

Across South Asia, specialists on violence (military and paramilitary commanders) are the principal agents of the government. Like their colonial predecessors, these specialists are responsible for safeguarding the existing political and economic order through violence and coercion. Indeed, military and paramilitary forces in the subcontinent (especially in India, Pakistan and Bangladesh) are the successors of the colonial British Indian Army and different paramilitary units deployed by the British Raj.[8] And to this day, these forces carry the structure, organisation and tradition of an imperial military which was designed to dominate and repress the native population of the colony. Since the end of the Raj, these forces have emerged as the saviours of the post-colonial order which is based on the militarism of the ruling elite, as opposed to lofty democratic ideals espoused in the different constitutions adopted by the post-colonial states. The constitution may well be the founding document of the ostensibly democratic republic, but it is also the key document that is often used by the ruling elite to legitimise crimes which are perpetrated by armed and uniformed agents of the republic.

That the Indian government annually celebrates the adoption of the Indian constitution with a grand military parade in Delhi of course does not come as a surprise. It also does not come as a surprise that some opponents of the Indian state are also among the staunchest critics of its constitution. One of them was Cherukuri Rajkumar, the spokesperson of the Communist Party of India (Maoist). As Rajkumar wrote a few weeks before his own extrajudicial execution by a police death squad in July 2010:

In which part of India is the constitution prevailing...? In Dantewada, Bijapur, Kanker, Narayanpur, Rajnandgaon? In Jharkhand, Orissa? In Lalgarh, Jangalmahal? In the Kashmir Valley? Manipur? Where was your constitution hiding for 25 long years after thousands of Sikhs were massacred? When thousands of Muslims were decimated? When *lakhs* of peasants are compelled to commit suicide? When thousands of people are murdered by state-sponsored Salwa Judum gangs? When *adivasi* women are gang raped? When people are simply abducted by uniformed goons?[9]

In the national security state, 'uniformed goons' or specialists on violence are the heroes and experts, who are routinely celebrated and venerated through military parades, gallantry awards and commemorative events. They are the members of a special and separate class of praetorian elite in the society – a class that is created and sustained by the government through overt and covert militarisation of all the major areas of national life. This special status of the military and their efforts of militarisation are enabled not only by political leaders but also by mainstream media, civil society and big businesses. Across South Asia, campaigns of state terror are bolstered through overt and covert partnerships between the military, the government, media and civil society.

The image of the soldier as the hero and saviour is recurrent in South Asian media, especially when it comes to the coverage of internal wars or terror campaigns. Across the subcontinent, television broadcasts, news articles and opinion pieces routinely present these wars as essential and heroic missions undertaken by military and paramilitary forces.[10] On the other hand, the targets (or victims) of these missions are constantly dehumanised as epitomes of sinister evil. In the mainstream narrative of state terror campaigns, there are two sets of characters: agents of the state as heroes and enemies of the state (or society) as villains. This is despite the fact that these heroes and villains often perpetrate the same or similar crimes. Even when state crimes are perpetrated against non-violent or peaceful opponents or critics of the state, the victims are often described by the media as 'anti-nationals' or 'subversives' – in other words, villains in need of 'neutralisation' or 'conditioning' (words preferred by South Asian national security agencies) by agents of the state.

For the specialists on violence in South Asia, engineering such media narrative is a critical step towards ensuring public endorsement for state crimes while generating widespread condemnation for crimes against the state. This narrative is manufactured through an active collaboration between the national security establishment and nationalist media outlets, who are keen to carry out their patriotic duties by acting as pimps and propagandists of state terror. In this equation, dissenting journalists and intellectuals – like Najam Sethi in Pakistan or Arundhati Roy in India – who threaten or disturb the mainstream narrative, are invariably labelled by their own colleagues as 'anti-nationals', 'foreign agents' or 'traitors'.[11] And sometimes these dissidents – like Saleem Shahzad in Pakistan or Seema Azad in India themselves become victims of judicial persecution, abduction, torture or extrajudicial execution for their failure to respect the limits of dissent.[12]

In Sri Lanka, this was the equation that rendered dissident journalists like Poddala Jayantha and Prageeth Eknaligoda as enemies of the state. They became targets of Sri Lanka's white van death squads for their failure to respect and reproduce the national war narrative. This was at a time when many Sri Lankan journalists (working for pro-government news outlets) emerged as vocal cheerleaders of the Sri Lankan army and the Rajapaksa regime.[13] For these journalists, the Sri Lankan security forces and their commander-in-chief were the saviours of the motherland who had defeated the diabolical terrorists of the LTTE – an achievement worthy of unquestioned celebration and the endorsement of the Sri Lankan media. During the civil war and in its aftermath, Sri Lankan journalists – with many notable and honourable exceptions – indeed became loyal propagandists and apologists of the Sri Lankan government and its security forces. Aided and coordinated by the media relations wing of the Sri Lanka Army, their war propaganda involved the systematic portrayal of Tamil rebels as a cult of deviant murderers, unworthy of treatment according to the laws of war. This demonisation was crucial for justifying Sri Lankan war crimes and crimes against humanity.[14]

Media demonisation of the internal enemy – LTTE rebels in Sri Lanka, Balochis in Pakistan, Naxals in India, *maobadi*s in Nepal or *sharbahara*s in Bangladesh – is a recurrent feature of state terror campaigns. And recruiting journalists as pimps of terror is a core function carried out by the propaganda engineers of the national security state. In both Pakistan and Bangladesh, this function is primarily carried out by the Inter Services Public Relations (ISPR) agency – the public relations and propaganda wing of the military. In Pakistan, the ISPR (led by a general of the Pakistan Army) is currently responsible for ensuring favourable media coverage of counter-insurgency operations in Balochistan and Khyber Pakhtunkhwa. In Bangladesh, the ISPR (led by a civilian bureaucrat) is responsible for manufacturing a media narrative in which the armed forces (especially the army) are constantly lauded as patriotic saviours of the motherland. Also, the media relations wing of the Rapid Action Battalion is responsible for presenting crossfire killings as heroic actions against suspected criminals. In India, favourable media coverage of counter-insurgency operations in Kashmir, the Red Corridor and the north-east is engineered by the propaganda wings of different paramilitary forces. Indeed, the embedding of journalists within CRPF units is now a routine feature of Indian counter-insurgency campaigns in the Red Corridor.[15]

Apart from the official public relations (propaganda) organs, South Asian national security agencies are also responsible for covertly recruiting and deploying journalists in the service of internal wars.[16] These agencies – the ISI in Pakistan, the DGFI in Bangladesh and RAW and the IB in India – rely on a group of embedded 'natsec reporters' to plant stories in mainstream media that advance the 'national interest' and bolster national security narratives.[17] These natsec (national security) reporters, in other words, are often the unofficial stenographers or spokesmen of terror and power.

Across the subcontinent, the covert militarisation of the media is engineered through two groups of people: loyal journalists who embed themselves within the national security machinery and retired military officers and security bureaucrats who moonlight as pre-eminent national security experts (go-to sources for the media in all matters related to security, counter-insurgency or internal wars). These retired officers and bureaucrats are also the stewards of ostensibly independent civil society groups and the strategic think-tanks that advocate for military solutions in times of national crisis. Even after retirement, they carry on fighting the internal enemy by developing intellectual frameworks of internal wars that justify state crimes in the name of 'internal security' and the 'national interest'.

In India, one of the most influential national security think-tanks is the Institute for Conflict Management, which focuses on the 'continuous appraisal of internal security and the state's responses in all areas of existing or emerging conflicts in South Asia.'[18] The institute was founded in 1997 by KPS Gill – the infamous 'Butcher of Punjab', the chief architect of the brutal police crackdown against Sikh secessionists. Through public advocacy campaigns (organising events, producing policy papers/journals, arranging media interviews, publishing newspaper columns, etc.), the institute bolsters the Indian government's militarisation efforts and develops popular justifications for state terror campaigns across the country, especially in the Red Corridor and the seven sister states. Such think-tanks – proponents of the 'national interest', as opposed to the 'anti-national' human rights groups – are integral nodes in the core network of power elite in the post-colonial society. It is a network that is often referred to as the military-intelligence-media complex.

In South Asia, state terror campaigns are also enabled by the military-religious complex or nexus. Across the subcontinent, religion is often militarised in the service of internal wars. This is yet another mechanism inherited by post-colonial states from the British Raj, that organised the British Indian Army according to religious identities of native soldiers – in the process, defining some ethno-religious groups as 'martial races'.[19] After the end of the Raj, post-colonial armies not only emerged as the saviours of the state and nation but also as the guardians or protectors of the majority religion and ethnicity. The South Asian soldier not only serves and saves the state but also fights in the name of God. In Pakistan, for example, the official motto of the Pakistan Army (one of the successors of the British Indian Army) is *'iman, taqwa, jihad fi sabilillah'* (faith in Allah, fear of Allah, *jihad* for Allah).[20]

Militarisation of religion has always been a feature of state terror campaigns in Pakistan, where the nexus between the military and religious groups remain strong.[21] In 1971, the genocide in East Pakistan was justified by the military and the Islamic clergy as a *jihad* against Bengali Hindus. This was the primary justification that encouraged and enabled members of Islamist groups in the province to join al Badr (an allusion to the Battle of Badr, the first war fought by the Prophet Muhammad and his followers) – a death squad that abducted, tortured and executed secular Bengali intellectuals, in the name of saving Islam from 'miscreants' sponsored by India.[22]

After the secession of East Pakistan, the military regime of General Zia-ul-Haq engineered a massive campaign of Islamisation that irreversibly transformed the Pakistani state, where the army and national security agencies like the ISI became the principal guardians of Islam.[23] This campaign of Islamisation involved the creation and sponsorship of militant Islamist groups by the ISI. With the active backing of the CIA, many of these groups were then deployed in neighbouring Afghanistan, against the godless Soviets. In a blowback, some of these groups – as part of the TTP – are now waging a *jihad* against the Pakistani state and the army. Religion, in other words, can often become the Achilles' heel of the national security state.

Elsewhere in South Asia, the militarisation of Buddhism was a key feature of the Sri Lankan government's war against the LTTE. After the war, the Rajapaksa regime's continual sponsorship of nationalist Buddhist monks resulted in the rise of the Bodu Bala Sena (Buddhist Power Force), one of the most virulent Buddhist supremacist organisations in the world (which include the military-sponsored 969 movement, led by the 'mad monks' of Burma).[24] In Nepal, the Royal Nepalese Army (RNA) was responsible for protecting 'the only Hindu kingdom in the world', until the overthrow of the monarchy in 2006.[25] In Bangladesh, as part of their martial law regimes, both General Ziaur Rahman and General Hussain Muhammad Ershad transformed the state through Islamisation campaigns.[26] It was under the command of General Ershad that the Bangladesh Army carried out brutal counter-insurgency operations in the Chittagong Hill Tracts, in the name of protecting Bengali Muslim settlers from non-Muslim *jummas*.[27]

Even in ostensibly secular India, the national security bureaucracy is dominated by proponents of *Hindutva* (Hindu nationalism), who are driven by a vision of turning their country into a 'Hindu superpower' and a mission of saving Hindus from 'Muslim terrorists'.[28] One of the key reasons touted by the Indian national security establishment for deploying the Rashtriya Rifles in Jammu and Kashmir is the protection of Hindus (especially Kashmiri pandits) from Kashmiri Muslim 'infiltrators' sponsored by Pakistan.[29] For their part, the Kashmiri Hindus remain the staunchest supporters of terror campaigns in their state. The protection of the majority religion and ethno-religious group is one of the most recurrent justifications of state terror campaigns in the subcontinent.

Across South Asia, where specialists on violence are the saviours of the state and the majority religion, governments allocate colossal military budgets (euphemistically called defence budgets) to sponsor ever-expansive networks of armed forces, paramilitary units and national security agencies. These budgets invariably bolster the state's military machinery at the expense of ordinary citizens – budgets that cover the costs associated with maintaining deadly arsenals of tanks, missile launchers and combat aircrafts; budgets that divert public funds which could be used for building schools and hospitals.[30] Across the subcontinent, military commanders and their families also benefit from the system of Milbus – a system of economic exploitation and resource transfer that guarantees the military's position as one of the most pampered and privileged classes of the society, with unfettered access to some of the best medical facilities (exclusive military hospitals) and educational institutions (including military-sponsored schools and colleges).

In Bangladesh, officially one of the least developed countries in the world, where millions of people live in abject poverty without access to basic public goods such as education, employment or healthcare, the government each year allocates more than a billion dollars to sustain the national security machinery. Of course, each dollar allocated to the military budget is a dollar taken away from public funds which are used to fulfill citizens' rights to education, healthcare and other public goods. In 2014, the Bangladeshi government allocated BDT152 billion (US$1.96 billion) to its military budget.[31] Despite being one of the poorest countries in the world, Bangladesh has one of the most well-equipped militaries in South Asia, with more than 157,000 troops: 126,000 in the army, 16,900 in the navy and 14,000 in the air force.[32] Military officers and commanders are of course among the most privileged citizens of Bangladesh, enjoying hundreds of exclusive perks and privileges offered by the government. They are also the stewards of Bangladesh's Milbus (*fouji banijjo*, in Bengali). Like its counterparts in Pakistan and Sri Lanka, the Bangladesh Army is one of the biggest conglomerates in Bangladesh. It is a business empire worth more than US$500 million that includes five-star hotels, banks, cement factories, food processing plants, dairy farms, textile mills, shopping centres and hundreds of other ventures.[33]

In Bangladesh, Pakistan and Sri Lanka, specialists on violence are among the most influential economic actors in the society. They are also the predominant group of public administrators. In these three countries, the militarisation of civil administration is a recurrent phenomenon.[34] This militarisation primarily takes place through the appointment of military officers as civil bureaucrats, especially in positions or roles that involve administering the state's machinery of social control and managing the essential public services and utilities. In a large number of cases, military officers are also deputed to serve as diplomats, representing the state before foreign governments and international organisations. In the national security state, military officers are the most powerful group of civil servants, responsible for overseeing the most crucial functions of the government.[35] The military, in other words, is often the de facto decision maker in the ostensibly civilian bureaucracy. This bureaucracy is invariably used to coordinate state terror campaigns, which involve the mobilisation of the state's resources to sponsor internal wars and the proliferation of policy prescriptions to legitimatise such wars. An elaborate and expansive bureaucracy of state terror, dominated by specialists on violence, is a permanent fixture of the post-colonial state.

Also recurrent in the post-colonial state is the militarisation of education, that primarily serves two correlated purposes: venerating 'war heroes' and soldiers through textbooks; and preparing new generations of specialists on violence. The fact that becoming a specialist on violence by pursuing a career in the military (also, in the police) remains one of the most promising and enticing prospects for millions of young South Asians is not surprising. Every year, thousands of young Bangladeshis, Indians, Nepalis, Pakistanis and Sri Lankans queue in front of military recruitment centres, with the dream of joining the privileged class of the praetorian elite. The machinery of state terror of course needs young blood in the form of new recruits. And that is why cadet colleges (sponsored and administered by the military) in Bangladesh and Pakistan that start preparing young children (as young as 12) for an eventual military career remain among the best educational institutions. For many of these children and their parents, a career as an armed and uniformed saviour of the state, indeed, is the only ticket to upward mobility in a brutally unequal society.

Specialists on violence are the second pillar of the system of state terror in South Asia. They are the celebrated heroes and saviours of the post-colonial national security state. It is a state and a system where internal wars and terror campaigns are carried out with the active support and sponsorship of the political class, big businesses, the media, civil society and religious institutions. Of course, it is through such support, endorsement and sponsorship of the core network of power elite, that these specialists develop and administer the machinery of state terror, which is deployed against internal enemies who are dehumanised not only through black laws but also through manufactured media narratives, relentless terror-mongering by strategic think-tanks and edicts issued by the guardians of the majority religion and ethnicity. Across South Asia and elsewhere, the 'uniformed goons' of the republic may well abduct and execute people in secret, however, the same goons also valiantly march through the capital of the republic every year in the name of the 'national interest' and 'internal security'.

9

INTERNATIONAL SYSTEM
OF STATE TERROR

It was the birth of a new international political order. In 1945, between April and June, 850 delegates from 50 countries gathered in the city of San Francisco for an international conference which was sponsored by China, the Soviet Union, the United Kingdom and the United States.[1] The agenda of this conference was charting the way forward for a new international system that would replace the old world order. It was at this conference, which began on 25 April, that the charter of the United Nations was discussed and agreed upon by states united against the Axis powers (Germany, Italy and Japan).[2] After weeks of intense negotiations, the delegations reached an agreement regarding the final draft of the charter, which was officially signed by the delegates on 26 June.

In a speech delivered during the closing session of the conference, President Harry S. Truman thanked the delegates:

The charter of the United Nations which you have just signed is a solid structure upon which we can build a better world. History will honor you for it. Between the victory in Europe and the final victory in Japan, in this most destructive of all wars, you have won a victory against war itself.[3]

A few weeks later, at the beginning of August 1945, Truman ordered the nuclear annihilation of Hiroshima and Nagasaki.[4] The charter for 'a better world', indeed, was followed by the atomic bombs, ostensibly used 'to shorten the agony of war [and] to save the lives of thousands and thousands of young Americans.'[5] On 24 October, the United Nations officially came into existence as its charter legally entered into force. Since then, the primary responsibility for maintaining international peace and security has been assigned to the five permanent members (with veto powers) of the United Nations Security Council – the United States, the United Kingdom, Russia (erstwhile Soviet Union), France and China.[6]

This is the international system that now dictates our lives. A system that was originally designed to halt the return and rise of old national security states – like Nazi Germany and Fascist Italy – that thrived on war, aggression and repression. As the United Nations Charter declares, this system was designed 'to save succeeding generations from the scourge of war' by maintaining international peace and security; by developing friendly relations between states (based on the principles of equal rights and self-determination of people); by achieving international cooperation; and by promoting human rights and fundamental freedoms for all. The charter also sets out the basic principles on which the current world order is essentially based: sovereignty of the state; peaceful settlement of international disputes; territorial integrity and political independence of the state; and non-intervention in any matter that falls under the domestic jurisdiction of the state.

These are the basic principles that also shape the international human rights system, which is based on an expansive body of international human rights law.[7] Since 1948, in order to fulfil the promise of 'human rights and fundamental freedoms for all', members of the United Nations enacted a series of international treaties and declarations that would guarantee the civil, political, economic, social and cultural rights of people across the globe, irrespective of their race, sex, language or religion.[8] Some of these treaties were specifically designed to address horrific state crimes (like genocide) that were symptomatic of the old national security state.[9] These treaties were touted as the strongest possible international response to the unspeakable atrocities ('barbarous acts which have outraged the conscience of mankind') of Nazi Germany and its client states. The international human rights system, in other words, was ostensibly designed to engender a new era of international law that would replace the old order of repression with a new order of human security, rights and freedom. As the much celebrated Universal Declaration of Human Rights put it, this was a promise of 'the advent of a world in which human beings shall enjoy freedom of speech and belief and freedom from fear and want.'

Despite the lofty promises, the international human rights system offers little or no recourse to the millions of people across the globe, who become the victims of state crimes perpetrated by their own governments. These victims of state terror neither have freedom from fear (as in freedom from violence by agents of the state) nor do they enjoy freedom from want (as in freedom from structural violence in the form of economic exploitation, hunger and poverty). As opposed to traditional wars between states, they are scourged by internal 'dirty wars' and 'security crackdowns'.[10] State terror in our time is perpetrated under the very system that was ostensibly designed in response to the crimes of old national security states.[11]

In the international system, the existence of new national security states and campaigns of terror carried out by their specialists on violence are facilitated by two major contradictions or paradoxes inherent in the United Nations Charter and international human rights law. These two contradictions, in effect, enable an international system of state terror. Since the end of the Second World War, this system of terror has been responsible for the emergence of post-colonial national security states in Latin America, Africa, Southeast Asia, South Asia and other regions of the world.

When it comes to state terror and state crimes, the first contradiction is between the paramount principle of respecting state sovereignty (also, domestic jurisdiction) and the lofty promise of protecting fundamental human rights. In this equation, state crimes are indeed crimes of sovereignty – a phenomenon that, by design, remains largely ignored or unaddressed in international law. This, primarily, is resultant from a focus on 'individual criminal responsibility' and a lack of any legal definition of state crimes.[12] International human rights law assigns the primary responsibility of protecting human rights to the very institution – the state – that is most often the biggest abuser of these rights. This is a paradoxical legal arrangement in which the sponsors and perpetrators of state crimes are also responsible for ensuring security and justice for the victims of these crimes. For these victims, the agents of violence and oppression are also the pre-appointed administrators of human security. The fact that the governments who have signed and ratified international human rights treaties are also prolific in enacting black laws that violate these very treaties of course comes as no surprise. To borrow a phrase from computer science, this indeed is a feature of the system, not a bug.

In exceptional or extraordinary circumstances, international law does recognise the need to protect people from 'widespread or systematic' state crimes (or, more accurately, a state's failure to protect people from such crimes), through coercive measures including economic sanctions and military interventions. In recent years, this question of the international protection of human rights has been addressed through the concept or doctrine of R2P (Responsibility to Protect).[13] R2P is a legal and political mechanism in which responsibility of protecting people across the globe from widespread and systematic state crimes (genocide, ethnic cleansing, war crimes and crimes against humanity) is assigned to the United Nations Security Council, especially the five permanent members of the council: China, France, Russia, the United Kingdom and the United States.[14] That these five states (known as the P5) are also the principal sponsors of the international system or network of state terror is the second contradiction or paradox – a contradiction between responsibility of protecting people from state crimes and sponsoring the very machinery of these crimes. This is yet another paradoxical arrangement, in which the pre-appointed international protectors of human rights are also the key sponsors of human rights abuses.

The leading sponsors of the international system of state terror – and, the custodians of international peace and security – are themselves responsible for horrific war crimes and crimes against humanity, perpetrated as part of internal terror campaigns and external wars. To mention a few of the most infamous cases: China in Tibet and Xinjiang; France in Algeria; Russia in Chechnya; the United Kingdom in Kenya and Northern Ireland; and the United States in Vietnam, Iraq and Afghanistan. Noteworthy here is the fact that the tools, technologies and strategies of terror which were first developed by these core national security states are now used by their client states in the peripheries of the world capitalist system.[15] Indeed, the primary function of the international network of state terror is unrestrained and unfettered distribution or diffusion of these tools, technologies and strategies, in the name of military cooperation and counter-terrorism partnerships.[16]

In its current form, the international system of state terror is a branch of the international political and economic system. It is an integral part of the new world order that emerged after the Second World War. It was under the new international order established through the United Nations that the core countries of the world also created a new economic order stewarded by the International Monetary Fund (IMF), the World Bank (WB) and the World Trade Organization (WTO). These organisations revised and updated the rules of the world capitalist system, replacing the old colonial order with a new system of massive economic exploitation of the peripheral states – exploitation bolstered through massive campaigns of terror and repression.[17] And this new system (based on the principles of unrestrained capitalism and unfettered trade) facilitates the international trade in tools of terror – a system that has clearly triumphed over the so-called international human rights system.

Indeed, the international system or network of state terror – through which sponsor states transfer tools and technologies of terror to client states – is an example of friendly relation, cooperation and free trade between nations. It is relation, cooperation and trade in the form of military ties, counter-terrorism alliances and arms transfer. This, of course, is the system that facilitates a continual partnership between the different national security states; a system that brings together specialists on violence from Bangladesh and other countries, through military conferences like PASOC; a system that enables a massive transfer of weapons from countries like China, Israel and the United States to recipients like Sri Lanka, India and

Pakistan; a system that allows outsourcing of torture by the United Kingdom to Pakistan; a system that involves US-sponsored training of Nepalese army officers. And this system or network is the third pillar of state terror in South Asia and other parts of the globe.

In corporate or business terms, the international system of state terror can also be described as a franchising operation, in which different states are part of different franchises of terror. That is to say, at the global level, the business of state terror is always dependent on the relationship between the sponsor (franchiser) states and the affiliate (franchisee) states. In our world, without exception, terror is perpetrated by states that are either affiliated with global or regional hegemons or that are hegemons themselves. In this business model, torture centres and secret detention facilitates run by Third World death squads are invariably connected to the international network of terror – not only serving the national security state and its ruling elite, but also serving the strategic interests (military, political and economic) of sponsor states. Repression in the peripheral states is always correlated to systemic exploitation by the core states – this, indeed, is a key feature of the international political economy of state terror. The international system or franchise of state terror is the dark underbelly of what is often called the 'global security structure', which is designed to protect the international order from major threats that include transnational terrorism and organised crime.[18]

Since the end of the Second World War, this global security structure has been developed by the P5 states, as part of two 'global civil wars' or global states of exception: the Cold War (1947–1991) and the post-9/11 war on terror (2001–present). During the Cold War, the great powers engaged in 'proxy wars' against each other by developing a common model of terror franchising (also known as security cooperation) that enabled their Third World affiliates to wage 'dirty wars' against internal enemies. This model was revised, updated and further developed as part of the war on terror. This, of course, is an integral part of the global security structure or system that has three key functions: the international transfer or exchange in tools of terror (military aid, arms transfer, counter-terrorism training etc.); political sponsorship and cooperation at the global level (especially at the United Nations); and deployment of soldiers from Third World national security states as peacekeepers in failed or failing states – in effect, as mercenaries of global or regional order.[19]

At the regional level, within the South Asian 'security structure', India has emerged as a hegemon that not only deploys death squads against its own people but also sponsors state terror in other client states – Bangladesh, Nepal and Sri Lanka. In Bangladesh, Indian sponsorship in the form of military and intelligence training gave birth to the Jatiyo Rakkhi Bahini in 1972. In recent years, India has emerged as the main international sponsor of the Hasina regime.[20] In Nepal, India had armed and trained the Royal Nepalese Army since the beginning of the Nepalese civil war. The Indian government also opposed and blocked the effective monitoring of the war by international organisations, by describing the conflict as Nepal's 'internal matter' (domestic jurisdiction). In Sri Lanka, between 1987 and 1990, India deployed a 'peace keeping force' (IPKF) to assist the Sri Lankan war effort against the LTTE. As part of the IPKF, thousands of Indian military and paramilitary troops were sent to the island in an effort to disarm LTTE rebels. These 'peacekeepers' then engaged in terrible human rights abuses and war crimes against Tamil civilians and suspected rebels: widespread rape of Tamil women; massacres; indiscriminate shelling and strafing of civilian areas; and enforced disappearance, torture and extrajudicial execution.[21]

Despite its sorry record of 'peacekeeping' in Sri Lanka and allegations of brutal human rights abuses at home, India is now one of the largest troop contributors to United Nations peacekeeping missions across the globe. In March 2015, more than 8,000 Indian military and police personnel were serving as UN peacekeepers in 12 different missions.[22] To date, more than 100,000 Indian troops have served in peacekeeping missions in different corners of the world.[23] These Indian 'blue helmets' (nickname for peacekeepers) often engaged in abuses (primarily sexual abuses) in their host countries, in blatant violation of the human rights guidelines and standards set by the United Nations.[24] Even so, the Indian government is now campaigning for permanent membership of the United Nations Security Council, by touting its status as one of the leading saviours of global peace and order.[25] This Indian bid for Security Council membership is of course opposed by China, the other regional hegemon and emerging superpower (also, one of the P5).[26]

Chinese sponsorship of state terror in South Asia began as early as 1971, when the Chinese delegation at the Security Council defended Pakistani atrocities in East Pakistan by describing Pakistani war crimes and crimes against humanity against Bengalis as 'internal matters' that fell under Pakistan's 'domestic jurisdiction'. Since then, China has backed successive military regimes in Pakistan through the massive transfer of weapons that are now being used against Pakistan's internal enemies. Pakistan's dirty war against Baloch nationalists is of course serving a Chinese strategic interest in the country, that is, the development of a deep-sea port near Gwadar, as part of a new China–Pakistan 'silk road'.[27]

Another planned deep-sea port near the town of Hambantota (in southern Sri Lanka) was one of the major reasons behind the Chinese sponsorship of the Rajapaksha regime during and after the Sri Lankan civil war.[28] In Sri Lanka, China not only fuelled the war by arming the Sri Lankan military through generous arms export but it also provided political cover to the regime at the United Nations by repeatedly citing Sri Lanka's 'domestic jurisdiction' and its 'sovereign right' to defeat a terrorist organisation. Sri Lanka's version of the 'war on terror' was also supported by Pakistan and Israel, through arms transfer and counter-insurgency training.

Such counter-insurgency and counter-terrorism partnerships are indeed used by the United States and the United Kingdom for sponsoring dirty wars and human rights abuses in their client states. In South Asia, this has been most visible in Pakistan where the United States invested millions of dollars in sponsoring the country's machinery of terror, in the name of fighting the Taliban and al Qaeda. Elsewhere, the United States generously supported the Royal Nepalese Army (during the Nepalese civil war) and the Bangladeshi military (as part of the 'war on terror'), primarily through its IMET programme.

According to a report by the Congressional Research Service, the US Pacific Command 'views Bangladesh as a "strong partner who works closely with the U.S. to enhance regional security."'[29] Between 2009 and 2011, the United States provided military and counter-terrorism assistance to Bangladesh worth more than US$15 million: US$3 million as foreign military financing; US$2 million in the form of IMET training; and US$10 million as part of 'nonproliferation, antiterrorism, demining and related programs.'[30] According to leaked US diplomatic cables, most of these military aid programmes (planned as early as in 2006) were aimed towards 'improving Bangladeshi counter-terrorism capabilities.'[31] A stumbling block in US counter-terrorism aid to Bangladesh, however, has been the Rapid Action Battalion's (RAB) notoriety as a death squad. Due to the Leahy law (which bars the United States government from providing military assistance to foreign military units engaged in human rights abuses), the United States refrained from directly entering into a partnership with the RAB, even though it is the leading counter-terrorism unit in Bangladesh.[32]

Such legal limitations, however, did not stop the British government from 'training RAB for 18 months in areas such as investigative interviewing techniques and rules of engagement.'[33] The fact that the United Kingdom had been training a Bangladeshi death squad was first reported by *The Guardian* in December 2010. As noted in the report, which was primarily based on leaked US diplomatic cables and interviews with government officials:

> there have been disagreements within the Foreign Office about the British government's involvement with the RAB. Some officials have argued that the partnership with the RAB is an essential component of the UK's counter-terrorism strategy in the region, while others have expressed concern that the relationship could prove damaging to Britain's reputation.[34]

Despite the concern about 'Britain's reputation', the British government did procure the services of a specialised torture centre in Bangladesh. As *The Guardian* revealed in January 2011, a number of British citizens were taken to the notorious Taskforce Interrogation Cell (TFI) in Dhaka, at the behest of MI5 and MI6.[35] This was yet another case of British intelligence agencies outsourcing their torture needs to South Asian specialists on violence.

In hindsight, Bangladesh's record of human rights abuses (especially torture and extrajudicial execution by the security forces) never stopped its military and paramilitary forces from entering into lucrative partnerships with international actors of high repute, including the United Nations. In recent years, Bangladesh has emerged as one of the top troop contributors to UN peacekeeping missions. In July 2015, more than 9,000 military and police personnel from Bangladesh were serving as peacekeepers in eleven different DPKO missions across the globe. This gave Bangladesh the first position in the monthly ranking of UN peacekeeping troop contributors. In the same month, more than 7,500 Pakistani peacekeepers were serving in seven missions, earning their country the fourth position in the ranking; second position went to Ethiopia with more than 8,000 troops; and third position went to India with more than 7,900 troops.[36]

It is not surprising that the United Nations recruits its peacekeepers from countries with terrible records of human rights abuses. The United Nations remains one of the major tools of global governance through which the great powers of our time pursue their strategic interests (political and economic) throughout the globe, even when such interests are served by dirty wars and campaigns of state terror. This, of course, is despite the promises of human rights and fundamental freedoms enshrined in the United Nations Charter, the founding document of a new global order dominated by the P5 countries. Since the end of the Second World War, these countries – the United States, the United Kingdom, Russia, France and China – have also been the key sponsors of the international system of state terror. And this indeed is the system that not only enables death squads in Third World national security states to roam the streets with impunity, but also protects repressive regimes in South Asia and across the globe in the name of 'state sovereignty', 'domestic jurisdiction' and the 'war on terror'.

10

A NOTE FROM THE
TORTURE CHAMBER

This was one of the most notorious torture chambers in Bangladesh. The windowless room was like an old recording studio, soundproofed with wooden panels on the walls. There were two CCTV cameras attached to the ceiling. Behind me was a metal bed frame with leather straps. The frame had a wheel, used for changing its angle and lifting it up or down. Right next to the bed, hanging from the ceiling were two wrist cuffs made of rubber or leather. Before me was a large wooden table with three batons on it. I was sitting on a wooden bench, relieved. Relieved because my torture session was over for then and they had taken off my blindfold. It was then I realised that being blindfolded was somehow more painful than getting beaten with batons from all sides. Or, was it really? The people who could offer me an informed answer had already left the room. Indeed, they were the pre-eminent experts on the science of pain and violence – my captors, officers of the Directorate General of Forces Intelligence (DGFI).

A few hours earlier, I had been picked up from my Central Road home in Dhaka. This was a little after midnight on May 11, 2007 – a few days before my 26th birthday. A group of armed men in plain clothes barged into my apartment and instructed me to go with them. Would they show me a warrant of arrest? I asked. 'We do not have to,' they said. 'There is a state of emergency.' At least they could tell me and my wife where they were taking me? I asked. 'You will see when we get there.' I kept insisting, like a dogged lawyer trying to save his client who had been sentenced to death. Only I was trying to save myself from a sinister journey into the dark abyss of that night. And then, one of them relented, 'You will be taken to the Sangshad Bhaban army camp.' I did not know there was an army camp in or near the parliament building. That would have been a trip to the parliament not as a citizen or a journalist, but as a detainee. His squirm gave it away – the agent of the state was lying.

Before they escorted me out, they took me to my study, and their leader – a young man who looked a bit like one of my distant cousins – sat down at my computer and started reading an email I was drafting. I told him, politely, that he was not supposed to read my emails without my permission. He did not even look up. I was never that keen on email privacy, however, watching a stranger going through my inbox, sitting on my chair, somehow ticked me off. A deep, nauseating sensation of disgust took over my body. I looked at my right hand, then, placed a finger on the reset button of the computer and pressed it. He instantly jumped up from the chair and pulled out a revolver from his holster. Pressing the cold tip of the gun on my lips, he started shouting, 'You are under arrest!' I started shouting back (something or other about the law). They all started shouting abuses at me and asking me to shut up. I looked towards the door – my wife was standing there, holding our six-month-old son. And both of them were watching, in silence. They watched, as I was led out of our apartment.

For the next few hours, whenever the suffocating blindfold sent shivers through my spine, I kept picturing my wife and my son – his eyes and her hair. It worked, it calmed me down, even when a group of strong, brave men surrounded me inside a windowless room and rained down slaps, punches, kicks and blows from all possible directions. I could not even move my handcuffed hands; they did not leave me any space. And I sat there, motionless, on a torture bench – inside the DGFI headquarters, in the middle of Dhaka cantonment. My country was in a state of emergency.

And under this state of emergency, some of the rights enshrined in the Bangladeshi constitution had been suspended: freedom of movement (Article 36); freedom of assembly (Article 37); freedom of association (Article 38); freedom of thought, conscience and speech (Article 39); freedom of profession or occupation (Article 40); and rights to property (Article 42).[1]

Four months earlier, in January 2007, the Bangladeshi military had carried out a bloodless coup and installed a puppet 'caretaker government' led by a former official of the World Bank. After more than a decade of democratic rule, the generals marched into the presidential palace in Dhaka and forced the president to declare a 'state of emergency'. With that declaration, military convoys came out of the cantonments and spread throughout the country. As *The Economist* described it, this was a 'guardian coup', modelled after military interventions in Fiji and Thailand.[2]

As it brought an end to fierce street battles between the two ever-feuding political camps (Bangladesh Nationalist Party and Awami League), the coup was welcomed by most of the socio-economic elite of the country. Among the most vocal and visible cheerleaders of the new regime were prominent members of the civil society and business leaders. Also cheerleading for the military were some of my journalist colleagues – reporters and editors – who started dreaming of a day when most of the Bangladeshi politicians would be sent behind bars and the uniformed messiahs would save the country from destruction. After a long wait, the saviours had arrived.

The saviours of course had international sponsors. The soft coup of January 2007 itself was partly engineered by senior officials of the United Nations. As *The Economist* noted in February 2007, it was a public statement by the United Nations' resident representative in Bangladesh that prodded the military to take charge of the country:

On January 11th, [the resident representative] gave warning in a public statement that if the Bangladeshi army proceeded to provide security for a dodgy election due on January 22nd, this might 'have implications' for its lucrative involvement in UN peacekeeping contracts. The UN's implicit threat had an immediate effect. The same day Lieutenant General Moeen U. Ahmed, the army chief, marched into the office of Bangladesh's president, Iajuddin Ahmed, and ordered him to declare a state of emergency, cancel the election, and install a military-backed caretaker government. The intervention was strange on the face of it, because the UN is not known to go around inciting army takeovers.[3]

This de facto army takeover in Bangladesh was quickly welcomed and endorsed by the United States and the United Kingdom. Indeed, US and British diplomats stationed in Dhaka had advance knowledge of the coup bid.[4]

Buoyed by domestic and international support, the army then set out to create a military-controlled political order by dismantling mainstream political parties. As part of its 'reform programme', the regime embarked on an 'anti-corruption drive' that resulted in the arrest and imprisonment of more than 400,000 people within a few months. Most of the detainees were members of different political parties. Soon, army-run torture centres started mushrooming across the country.

As Peter Lloyd, South Asia correspondent of the Australian Broadcasting Corporation, reported in June 2007:

An ABC investigation has uncovered evidence linking Bangladesh's military-backed government with mass arrests, illegal detention, torture and murders. Military-run interrogation centres operate all over the country. Some, such as Fatullah stadium on the outskirts of Dhaka, are brazenly open. [...] [A witness] described how he heard torture victims screaming in agony during a local cricket match. Later in the same day, a senior army officer boasted openly that suspects were far more talkative after they had been given electric shocks, beaten and subjected to water torture.[5]

This campaign of torture and terror – aimed towards establishing absolute and unquestioned military control over all the major areas of national life – was led by the DGFI, the agency that had the primary responsibility of 'neutralising' critics and political opponents of the military. It was in this context, I became an 'internal enemy' in my own country, primarily because of my reporting about torture and extrajudicial executions by the Rapid Action Battalion (RAB). Since the declaration of the state of emergency, I was also investigating cases of torture and extrajudicial executions perpetrated by the Bangladesh Army. My work as an investigative journalist and profile as a vocal critic of the military eventually drew in that small group of Bangladeshi specialists on violence to my door. They took me to the torture chamber, where I was detained for 22 hours: interrogated, verbally abused, tortured, forced to write and record false confessions.[6]

I was of course not the first person (or the first journalist) taken to a torture chamber in South Asia. Nor am I the last. Every year, countless numbers of people are 'processed' through thousands of torture facilities that are dotted throughout South Asian cities and towns. Many of them are eventually executed and their bodies thrown by the roadside. Some disappear forever, without any trace. Many are secretly buried or cremated in the name of 'national security' and 'public order'. How many have been executed by South Asian death squads? How many were tortured? How many are right now languishing in secret detention facilities? We will never know the exact numbers.

What we do know about are the socio-political conditions that bolster state terror in the post-colonial world: legacies of colonialism, structural violence, coercive governance and militarism. We know how black laws sanction the use of abduction, torture and execution as techniques of control and coercion. We know how specialists on violence are touted as saviours for their relentless butchery. We know how states of exception are created for sponsoring and authorising dirty wars and campaigns of terror. We know how the national security state thrives under an international system of state terror. And, what we know about the *jallad*, will enable us to plan our resistance against it – resistance aimed towards saving succeeding generations from the scourge of torture and extrajudicial execution.

This resistance must start with an opposition to black laws. Our politics for human rights and fundamental freedoms must deny our rulers any legal tool that can be used to rob us of our humanity and dignity, even during the worst of crises or gravest of emergencies (perceived or real). This is why it remains urgent to identify the black laws that sanction and authorise campaigns of terror in our societies. If we are to dismantle the system of state terror, we need to repeal its legal pillars one by one. We must also identify the leading specialists on violence in our societies and deny them the impunity they have been enjoying for decades. Here, we have to attack the institutions of militarism and work towards demilitarising our societies. We have to build new societies where butchers are not celebrated as saviours. And finally, we have to challenge regional and global hegemony that sponsors and perpetrates terror in our world. If we are to curtail the repressive power of the state, we must attack the coercive and exploitative world order that sustains the state. Ours should be a world where Reginald Dyers no longer march through the streets and torture chambers no longer exist.

NOTES

1. Introduction: After the Colony

1. In this chapter, my description of colonial Amritsar and the Jallianwala Bagh massacre is primarily based on: Nigel Collett, *The Butcher of Amritsar: General Reginald Dyer*. London: Hambledon, 2005.
2. Struggle against 'black laws' was one of the key pillars of Gandhi's philosophy of non-violence and civil disobedience. For an overview of this, see Erik H. Erikson, *Gandhi's Truth: On the Origins of Militant Nonviolence*. New York: Norton, 1993, pp. 383–89.
3. S. Nihal Singh, 'The Rowlatt Bills: A Native View', *The Observer*, 20 April 1919, available via ProQuest.
4. Mahatma Gandhi, *Gandhi: Selected Political Writings*. Indianapolis, IN: Hackett, 1996, p. 62.
5. Collett, *The Butcher of Amritsar*, pp. 260–61.
6. For a socio-political analysis of the massacre, see Helen Fein, *Imperial Crime and Punishment: The Massacre at Jallianwala Bagh and British Judgment, 1919–1920*. Honolulu, HI: University Press of Hawaii, 1977.
7. Collett, *The Butcher of Amritsar*, pp. 377–402.
8. Ibid., p. 431.
9. For a detailed discussion on the 'black laws of Punjab', see People's Union for Democratic Rights, 'Black Laws and the People: An Enquiry into the Functioning of Black Laws in Punjab', New Delhi, 1985, available via CSSH Project on Archiving Documents on Human Rights (University of Pune), at: www.unipune.ac.in/snc/cssh/HumanRights/index.html (accessed 22 September 2015).
10. Human Rights Watch, 'Dead Silence: The Legacy of Human Rights Abuses in Punjab', New York, 1994, pp. 1–2.
11. Joyce Pettigrew, 'Parents and their Children in Situations of Terror: Disappearances and Special Police Activity in Punjab', in Jeffrey Sluka (ed.), *Death Squad: The Anthropology of State Terror*. Philadelphia, PA: University of Pennsylvania Press, 2000, pp. 207–08.
12. Jyotsna Singh, 'Profile: KPS Gill', *BBC*, 8 May 2002.
13. S.P. Talukdar, 'Punjab's Gill Complex', *Business Standard*, 31 December 2013.
14. For an overview of the colonial origins of military rule in Pakistan, see Syed Soherwordi, '"Punjabisation" in the British Indian Army 1857–1947 and the Advent of Military Rule in Pakistan', *Edinburgh Papers in South Asian Studies* (24), 2010.

15. Stanley Maron, 'The Problem of East Pakistan', *Pacific Affairs* (28: 2), 1955, pp. 132–44.
16. For a profile of Yahya Khan and an overview of his politics, see Lawrence Ziring, 'Militarism in Pakistan: The Yahya Khan Interregnum', *Asian Affairs* (1: 6), 1974, pp. 402–20.
17. Helal Uddin Ahmed, 'Seventh March Address', *Banglapedia: National Encyclopedia of Bangladesh*. Dhaka: Asiatic Society of Bangladesh, 2012.
18. For an account, see International Commission of Jurists, 'The Events in East Pakistan, 1971: A Legal Study by the Secretariat of the International Commission of Jurists', Geneva, 1972, pp. 15–23.
19. Quoted in Sarmila Bose, 'Anatomy of Violence: Analysis of Civil War in East Pakistan in 1971', *Economic and Political Weekly* (40: 41), 2005, p. 4464.
20. My description of Operation Searchlight is primarily based on two sources: Siddiq Salik, *Witness to Surrender*. Karachi: Oxford University Press, 1977; and International Commission of Jurists, 'The Events in East Pakistan, 1971'.
21. International Commission of Jurists, 'The Events in East Pakistan, 1971', p. 27.
22. Ibid., pp. 29–30.
23. Ibid., p. 30.
24. For general and academic readers, I recommend two recently published books that cover the 1971 genocide in great detail, see Gary J. Bass, *The Blood Telegram: Nixon, Kissinger, and a Forgotten Genocide*. London: Hurst, 2014; and Srinath Raghavan, *1971: A Global History of the Creation of Bangladesh*. Cambridge, MA: Harvard University Press, 2013.
25. In Chapter 2, I note the large-scale deployment of three tools of terror: torture centres, 'rape camps' and al Badr death squad. See also Redress, 'Torture in Bangladesh 1971–2004', London, 2004, pp. 7–8.
26. Frantz Fanon, *The Wretched of the Earth*. London: Penguin, 2001 [1961], pp. 29, 138. This, indeed, is one of the most accurate descriptions of the post-colonial national security state.
27. Here, I am extending Jeffrey Sluka's definition of state terror, that is, 'the use or threat of violence by the state or its agents or supporters, particularly against civilian individuals and populations, as a means of political intimidation and control.' See Jeffrey Sluka (ed.), *Death Squad: The Anthropology of State Terror*. Philadelphia, PA: University of Pennsylvania Press, 2000, p. 2.
28. In discussing dehumanisation and state of exception, throughout this book, I am guided by two seminal works by Giorgio Agamben: *Homo Sacer: Sovereign Power and Bare Life*, translated by Daniel Heller-Roazen. Stanford, CA: Stanford University Press, 1998; and *State of Exception*, translated by Kevin Attell. Chicago, IL: University of Chicago Press, 2005.
29. Fanon, *Wretched of the Earth*, pp. 88, 103.
30. Ibid., pp. 109.
31. In 1941, Harold Lasswell predicted the emergence of 'garrison states', in which 'specialists on violence are the most powerful group in society.' In 1978, Lasswell's thesis was developed further by Martin Oppenheimer and Jane Canning. These two works, primarily, form the basis of my own discussion of the national security state. See Harold Lasswell, 'The Garrison State', *American*

Journal of Sociology (46: 4), 1941, pp. 455–68; Martin Oppenheimer and Jane C. Canning, 'The National Security State: Repression within Capitalism', *Berkeley Journal of Sociology* (23), 1978–1979, pp. 3–33.

32. For an overview, see Eqbal Ahmad, *The Selected Writings of Eqbal Ahmad*, Carollee Bengelsdorf, Margaret Cerullo and Yogesh Chandrani (eds). New York: Columbia University Press, 2006, pp. 107–59.

33. Fanon, *Wretched of the Earth*, p. 60.

34. Oppenheimer and Canning, 'National Security State', (see Note 31) discuss two types of national security state: 'Type I [...] which is typical of Third World, less-developed countries in the peripheral branches of the world capitalist mode of production.' 'Type II,' on the other hand, 'is typical of the developed core, "mother country" plus "sibling partner/rival" branches.'

35. Sluka, *Death Squad*, p. 9.

36. I define a death squad as an armed group – usually a military, paramilitary or special police unit – that perpetrates extrajudicial execution, enforced disappearance and torture, as part of a state terror campaign. According to a slightly different definition:

    > death squads [is] a term given to paramilitary units that are most often associated with or directly part of the security forces of a country. These units are used to eliminate a regime's perceived opponents, often in ways with which a regime is unwilling to be publicly associated. [...] Torture, arbitrary arrest and detention, disappearances, denial of a fair and public trial are but a few of the human rights violations associated with death squads.

    See Winston E. Langley, *Encyclopedia of Human Rights Issues Since 1945*. Westport, CT: Greenwood Press, 1999, p. 80.

37. *AS (s.55 'exclusion' certificate — process) Sri Lanka v Secretary of State for the Home Department*, 2013, UKUT 00571 (IAC), available via Refworld.

38. Immigration and Refugee Board of Canada, 'Sri Lanka: Information on Whether the "White Van" is Related to Rape, Torture and Killing and is Connected to the Army or Police; and on Any Incidents of "White Van" Killings in Colombo Since 1994', 1996, available via Refworld.

39. Manoj Poudel, 'Victim Reports Torture', *The Kathmandu Post*, 4 January 2013.

40. Trishna Rana, 'Commissions of Convenience', *Nepali Times*, 18–24 July 2014.

41. Leon Watson, 'British Police Charge Nepali Army Colonel with Two Counts of Torture during Himalayan Nation's Decade-Long Civil War', *Daily Mail*, 5 January 2013; Phanindra Dahal, 'UN No to Diplomatic Immunity for Colonel', *The Kathmandu Post*, 10 January 2013.

42. International Commission of Jurists, 'Nepal: The Case of Colonel Kumar Lama', Geneva, 2013.

43. Declan Walsh, 'Pakistan's Secret Dirty War', *The Guardian*, 29 March 2011.

44. Dan Morrison, 'Killings Made Him a Star', *Newsday*, 10 August 2004.

45. Zubair Ahmed, 'Bombay's Crack Encounter Police', BBC, 9 June 2004.

46. Tasneem Khalil, 'Justice, Bangladesh Style', *Forum* (1: 2), 2006.

2. Bangladesh: Men in Black

1. Sheldon W. Simon, 'US-Southeast Asian Relations: US Pushes Security and Trade Interests in Southeast Asia', *Comparative Connections* (8: 2), 2006, pp. 63–74.

2. According to Richard Strozzi-Heckler, a consultant who works with the US military:

   > The PASOC conference [gathers] military from over twenty nations in the Pacific Rim and Southeast Asia, as well as the U.S. military, State Department, CIA, FBI, NGOs, and AID. These conferences are groundbreaking in that they gather a diversity of nations and presenters that have never come together before, as well as build stronger communication among the different elements that need to coordinate around issues of counter-insurgency and counter-terrorism.

   See Richard Strozzi-Heckler, *In Search of the Warrior Spirit*. Berkeley, CA: Blue Snake Books, 2007, p. 416.

3. Ed Vulliamy and Antony Barnett, 'US Trained Butchers of Timor', *The Guardian*, 19 September 1999.

4. 'US Should Not Cozy Up to Kopassus: Notorious Military Unit Commander Participates in Hawaii Pentagon Conference', statement, East Timor and Indonesia Action Network, 6 April 2006.

5. Roy Tupai, 'US Criticized for Cozying Up to Kopassus', *Paras Indonesia* (via *Stop Wapenhandel*), 13 April 2006.

6. D.C. McCullough, 'Meeting with RAB A/DG: "Due Process is Our Objective"', leaked US diplomatic cable [05DHAKA2603], Dhaka, 6 June 2005, available via WikiLeaks.

7. As irony has it, the diplomats were visiting the RAB headquarters to 'present a box of books on legal matters (including the 2004 Country Human Rights Reports).'

8. Patricia A. Butenis, 'Former Commander Looks Back on RAB's Origins and Mission', leaked US diplomatic cable [06DHAKA2078], Dhaka, 13 April 2006, available via WikiLeaks.

9. In December 2006, I first used this phrase – 'men in black' – to describe the RAB in an article published by Forum. This was one of the earliest investigations into the RAB and its abuses. I also worked on a report published by Human Rights Watch that detailed torture and extrajudicial executions by the RAB. My discussion of the RAB in this chapter is primarily based on these works. See Tasneem Khalil, 'Justice, Bangladesh Style', *Forum* (1: 2), 2006; and Human Rights Watch, 'Judge, Jury, and Executioner: Torture and Extrajudicial Killings by Bangladesh's Elite Security Force', 2006.

10. Haroon Habib, 'Ruling with the Army', *Frontline*, 7–20 December 2002.

11. For an early account of Operation Clean Heart, see Jyoti M. Pathania, 'Bangladesh: Operation Clean Heart', South Asia Analysis Group (paper 674), 1 May 2003.

12. Human Rights Watch, 'Judge, Jury, and Executioner', pp. 16–17.
13. See Human Rights Watch, 'Judge, Jury, and Executioner', pp. 67–69; and M.I. Farooqui, 'Armed Police Battalions Ordinance, a Hybrid Law', *The Independent* (Bangladesh), 11 March 2005.
14. Telephone interview with a RAB commander in Dhaka (name withheld on request), December 2014.
15. This number is based on human rights monitoring statistics produced by Odhikar, at: odhikar.org (accessed March 2015). Since a large number of executions are not reported in the Bangladeshi press (a primary source for Odhikar's documentation), this should be considered as an estimate only.
16. Human Rights Watch, 'Judge, Jury, and Executioner', pp. 58–66.
17. This description of the torture of Sumon Ahmed Majumder is based on my own investigation of the case. See Khalil, 'Justice, Bangladesh Style'; and Human Rights Watch, 'Judge, Jury, and Executioner', pp. 35–39.
18. Khalil, 'Justice, Bangladesh Style'.
19. Human Rights Watch, 'Judge, Jury, and Executioner', p. 26.
20. This biographical sketch of Picchi Hannan is based on a case study of gangsters and petty criminals of Dhaka. See Imtiaz Ahmed, 'Mastanocracy, Violence and Chronic Poverty: Issues and Concerns', in Binayak Sen and David Hulme, *Chronic Poverty in Bangladesh: Tales of Ascent, Descent, Marginality and Persistence*. Dhaka: Bangladesh Institute of Development Studies (BIDS), 2004, p. 104.
21. This was one of the cases I investigated in depth. See Khalil, 'Justice, Bangladesh Style'.
22. For a discussion on the Maoist parties in Bangladesh, see Sumanta Banerji, 'Bangladesh's Marxist-Leninists: II', *Economic and Political Weekly* (17: 33), 1982, pp. 1311–13.
23. Before the creation of the RAB, *sarbahara*s were targeted by a vigilante death squad named Jagrata Muslim Janata Bangladesh (JMJB). This group was originally sponsored by a minister in Khaleda Zia's cabinet. JMJB killed at least 36 members of sarbahara parties in Rajshahi, Naogaon and Natore. In a curious turn of events, the group then declared a jihad against the Bangladesh government. In 2004, JMJB was banned as a terrorist organisation. See Khalil, 'Justice, Bangladesh Style'; Eliza Griswold, 'The Next Islamist Revolution?', *New York Times Magazine*, 23 January 2005; and 'Jagrata Muslim Janata Bangladesh (JMJB)', South Asia Terrorism Portal, at: satp.org (accessed March 2015).
24. This description of torture marks is primarily based on cases documented by Human Rights Watch (see Note 9).
25. Enforced disappearances are of course not new in Bangladesh, especially in the Chittagong Hill Tracts. See, for example, the case of Kalpana Chakma: Chris Chapman, 'Kalpana Chakma – Information, Disinformation, Non-Information', Amnesty International, 24 June 2014.
26. This is an estimate, based on human rights monitoring statistics produced by Odhikar, at: odhikar.org (accessed March 2015).
27. Some of these cases were rigorously investigated by journalists David Bergman and Muktadir Rashid. See David Bergman and Muktadir Rashid, 'Picked Up

a Year Ago, They are Yet to Return', *New Age*, 28 November 2014; 'How All It Began', *New Age*, 28 November 2014; 'They Picked Up 6 at Bashundhara and Drove Off', *New Age*, 30 November 2014; and 'I Will Investigate Allegations about 19 Disappearances: Law Minister', *New Age*, 5 December 2014.

28. For an account, see Meenakshi Ganguly, 'Dispatches: Forcibly Disappeared in Bangladesh', Human Rights Watch, 25 March 2015. Salahuddin Ahmed, the BNP leader mentioned in the article by Ganguly, was later found in India. See David Bergman and Muktadir Rashid, 'Anatomy of a Disappearance, and a Reappearance', *The Shillong Times*, 28 May 2015.

29. For background on the political situation in Bangladesh, see Lisa Curtis and Maneeza Hossain, 'Combating Islamism in South Asia: Keeping Bangladesh on the Democratic Path', The Heritage Foundation, 20 December 2013.

30. A.A.K. Niazi, 'From Counter-Insurgency to Defeat', in Meghna Guhathakurta and Willem van Schendel (eds), *The Bangladesh Reader: History, Culture, Politics*. Durham, NC: Duke University Press, 2013, pp. 244–46.

31. I am quoting an Urdu–English translation of '*main iss haramzadi qaum ki nasal badal doon ga.*' See Khaled Ahmed, '"Genetic Engineering" in East Pakistan', *The Express Tribune*, 7 July 2012.

32. See Redress, 'Torture in Bangladesh 1971–2004', London, 2004, p. 8; International Commission of Jurists, 'Events in East Pakistan, 1971: A Legal Study by the Secretariat of the International Commission of Jurists', Geneva, 1972, p. 40; and Nayanika Mookherjee, '"Remembering to Forget": Public Secrecy and Memory of Sexual Violence in the Bangladesh War of 1971', *The Journal of the Royal Anthropological Institute* (12: 2), 2006, pp. 433–50.

33. Redress, 'Torture in Bangladesh 1971–2004', p. 8.

34. My description of al Badr in this chapter is based on four sources: Husain Haqqani, *Pakistan: Between Mosque and Military*. Washington DC: Carnegie Endowment for International Peace, 2005, pp. 79–80; Seyed Vali Reza Nasr, *The Jamaat-i-Islami of Pakistan: The Vanguard of the Islamic Revolution*. Berkeley, CA: University of California Press, pp. 59, 133–34; International Commission of Jurists, 1972, pp. 44–45; and *The War Crimes File*, documentary, dir. Howard Bradburn, Twenty Twenty Television, UK, 1995.

35. *The War Crimes File*, 1995.

36. Muazzam Hussain Khan, 'Killing of Intellectuals', *Banglapedia: National Encyclopedia of Bangladesh*. Dhaka: Asiatic Society of Bangladesh, 2012.

37. Decades after independence, a special court in Bangladesh – the International Crimes Tribunal – is now trying some senior leaders of the BNP and Jamaat-e-Islami for their membership in al Badr and their participation in crimes against humanity in 1971. See Sabir Mustafa, 'Bangladesh's Watershed War Crimes Moment', *BBC*, 21 January 2013.

38. Anthony Mascarenhas, *Bangladesh: A Legacy of Blood*. London: Hodder and Stoughton, 1986, p. 36.

39. Mascarenhas, *Bangladesh: A Legacy of Blood*, p. 37.

40. Federal Research Division (Library of Congress), 'Bangladesh: A Country Study', 1989, p. 227.

41. Enamul Haq, 'Raksi Bahini', *Banglapedia: National Encyclopedia of Bangladesh.* Dhaka: Asiatic Society of Bangladesh, 2012.

42. Mascarenhas, *Bangladesh: A Legacy of Blood*, p. 37.

43. For an overview of the Special Powers Act of 1974, see Amnesty International, 'Bangladesh: Urgent Need for Legal and Other Reforms to Protect Human Rights', London, 2003.

44. Mascarenhas, *Bangladesh: A Legacy of Blood*, p. 45.

45. Ibid., p. 46.

46. For accounts of Mujib's assassination, see: Mascarenhas, *Bangladesh: A Legacy of Blood*, pp. 68–78; and Lawrence Lifschultz and Kai Bird, *Bangladesh: The Unfinished Revolution.* London: Zed Press, 1979.

47. See Talukder Maniruzzaman, 'Bangladesh in 1975: The Fall of the Mujib Regime and its Aftermath', *Asian Survey* (16: 2), 1976, pp. 119–29.

48. For a general overview of Rahman's politics, see Syed Serajul Islam, 'The State in Bangladesh under Zia (1975–81)', *Asian Survey* (24: 5), 1984, pp. 556–73.

49. Emajuddin Ahamed, 'Rahman, Shahid Ziaur', *Banglapedia: National Encyclopedia of Bangladesh.* Dhaka: Asiatic Society of Bangladesh, 2012.

50. Altaf Gauhar, 'How Intelligence Agencies Run our Politics', *The Nation* (Pakistan), 17 August 1997.

51. Human Rights Watch, 'The Torture of Tasneem Khalil', New York, 2008, p. 5.

52. See Veena Sikri, 'The Geopolitics of Bangladesh', *India Seminar*, (603), 2009.

53. Amnesty International, 'Report 1978', London, 1978, p. 148–52.

54. See N.M.J., 'Murder in Dacca: Ziaur Rahman's Second Round', *Economic and Political Weekly* (3: 12), 1978, pp. 551–58.

55. Rangan Kasturi, 'Bangladesh Leader is Shot and Killed in a Coup Attempt', *New York Times*, 31 May 1981.

56. For an Overview of Bangladesh's Political History, see Zillur R. Khan, 'Bangladesh's Experiments with Parliamentary Democracy', *Asian Survey* (37: 6), 1997, pp. 575–89.

57. For an overview of the history and politics of the CHT, see Naeem Mohaiemen (ed.), *Between Ashes and Hope: Chittagong Hill Tracts in the Blind Spot of Bangladesh Nationalism.* Dhaka: Dristipat Writers' Collective, 2010.

58. See Wolfgang Mey (ed.), *Genocide in the Chittagong Hill Tracts, Bangladesh.* Copenhagen: IWGIA, 1984.

59. See Hana Shams Ahmed, 'Part-Time Peacekeepers', *Himal*, 10 November 2014; and Kabita Chakma and Glen Hill, 'Indigenous Women and Culture in the Colonized Chittagong Hill Tracts of Bangladesh', in Kamala Visweswaran (ed.), *Everyday Occupations: Experiencing Militarism in South Asia and the Middle East.* Philadelphia, PA: University of Pennsylvania Press, 2013, pp. 132–57.

3. India: Brutal Encounters

1. In this chapter, my description (including this excerpt from an autopsy report) of the torture and execution of Thangjam Manorama Devi is based on two sources: Manorama Death Inquiry Commission (Justice Upendra Singh

Commission), 'Report of the Commission of the Judicial Inquiry', Manipur, 2004; and Human Rights Watch, 'These Fellows Must be Eliminated: Relentless Violence and Impunity in Manipur', New York, 2008.

2. Geeta Pandey, 'Woman at the Centre of Manipur Storm', *BBC*, 27 August 2004.
3. Human Rights Watch, 'These Fellows Must be Eliminated', p. 31.
4. Mihir Srivastava, 'The Siege Within: Manipur's Simmering Outrage', *Tehelka*, 2 September 2006.
5. For an organisational history, see D.K. Palit, *Sentinels of the North-East: The Assam Rifles*. New Delhi: Palit & Palit, 1984.
6. International Institute for Strategic Studies, 'Asia', *The Military Balance* (115: 1), 2015, p. 252.
7. The history of the Assam Rifles as a colonial army was first documented by Colonel L.W. Shakespear, one of the British commanders who oversaw the conquest of India's north-east, see Colonel L.W. Shakespear, *History of the Assam Rifles*. Calcutta: Firma KLM, 1929. See also Ian Heath and Michael Perry, *The North-East Frontier 1837–1901*. Oxford: Osprey Publishing, 1999.
8. For a brief overview, see Sumanta Banerjee, 'Indian State and its Armed Opponents', *Economic and Political Weekly* (35: 40), 2000, pp. 3573–75.
9. 'Poverty Rises in Northeast: Decline in Tripura, Arunachal; Increase in Assam, Nagaland, Manipur', *The Telegraph* (India), 20 March 2012.
10. Shubh Mathur, 'Life and Death in the Borderlands: Indian Sovereignty and Military Impunity', *Race & Class* (54: 1), 2012, pp. 33–49.
11. Operation Bluebird was the subject of an in-depth investigation by Amnesty International that focused on Assam Rifles abuses in Oinam. For a summary, see Clare Talwalkar, 'Security Forces Abuse Human Rights: AI Report on Oinam', *Economic and Political Weekly* (26: 3), 1991, pp. 89–90.
12. See People's Union for Democratic Rights, 'Army Atrocities in Naga Areas', New Delhi, 1987, available via CSSH Project on Archiving Documents on Human Rights (University of Pune).
13. Chinki Sinha, 'Just Another Massacre', *Open*, 25 May 2013.
14. R.K. Suresh, 'Irom Sharmila: Iron Lady Unshackled', *Tehelka*, 20 August 2014.
15. For a book-length profile of Irom Sharmila, see Deepti Priya Mehrotra, *Burning Bright: Irom Sharmila and the Struggle for Peace in Manipur*. New Delhi: Penguin, 2009.
16. These cases were meticulously documented by Manipuri human rights activists. See Simon Denyer, *Rough Elephant: Harnessing the Power of India's Unruly Democracy*. London: Bloomsbury, 2014, pp. 297–98.
17. Justice Santosh Hegde Commission, 'Report of the Supreme Court Appointed Commission', Manipur, 2013.
18. For an overview of these black laws, see Surabhi Chopra, *National Security Laws in India: The Unravelling of Constitutional Constraints*, research report, 2012, available via SSRN. See also C. Raj Kumar, 'Human Rights Implications of National Security Laws in India: Combating Terrorism While Preserving Civil Liberties', *Denver Journal of International Law and Policy* (33: 2), 2005, pp. 195–222.

19. For a summary of major cases of abuse and impunity (all sponsored through the act) in Manipur and Kashmir, see Mathur, 'Life and Death in the Borderlands', pp. 36–45.
20. Peace Direct, 'Kashmir: Conflict Profile', *Insight on Conflict*, at: insightonconflict. org (accessed March 2015).
21. Nitasha Kaul, 'Kashmir: A Place of Blood and Memory', *openDemocracy*, 31 August 2010.
22. This point is repeatedly made throughout the excellent collection of essays by Tariq Ali, Hilal Bhatt, Angana Chatterji, Pankaj Mishra and Arundhati Roy, which were published by Verso in 2011. Among these, I especially recommend the essay by Angana Chatterji, which deals with militarisation of Kashmir. Tariq Ali, *et al.*, *Kashmir: The Case for Freedom*. London: Verso, 2011.
23. Chatham House, 'Kashmir: Paths to Peace', London, 2010, pp. 15–16.
24. Ibid., p. 7.
25. Sachi Cunningham and Jigar Mehta, 'Kashmir: The Road to Peace?', *PBS Frontline/World*, November 2004.
26. Cathy Scott-Clark, 'The Mass Graves of Kashmir', *The Guardian*, 9 July 2012.
27. 'Defence Budget Hiked by 17.6 pc', *Indian Express*, 17 March 2012.
28. International Institute for Strategic Studies, 'Asia', p. 252. See also Gautam Navlakha, 'Shrinking Horizon of an Expanding Economy: India's Military Spending', *Economic and Political Weekly* (41: 14), 2006, pp. 1338–40.
29. For a discussion, see Gautam Navlakha, 'A Force Stretched and Stressed', *Economic and Political Weekly* (41: 46), 2006, pp. 4722–24.
30. International People's Tribunal on Human Rights and Justice in Indian administered Kashmir (IPTK), 'Buried Evidence. Unknown, Unmarked and Mass Graves in Indian-Administered Kashmir', Srinagar, 2009, p. 9.
31. These figures (of death and disappearance) are based on research published by the IPTK and other human rights organisations. See IPTK, 'Buried Evidence', p. 10.
32. The alleged killer of Andrabi, Major Avtar Singh, later immigrated to the United States. For an account, see Zahid Rafiq, 'From Kashmir to California: In the Footsteps of a Wanted Killer', *Christian Science Monitor*, 12 June 2012. See also Subh Mathur, 'Impunity in India', *Guernica*, 1 February 2013.
33. Scott-Clark, 'The Mass Graves of Kashmir'.
34. IPTK, 'Buried Evidence', pp. 10–18.
35. Ibid., pp. 69–83.
36. IPTK and Association of Parents of Disappeared Persons, 'Alleged Perpetrators: Stories of Impunity in Jammu and Kashmir', Srinagar, 2012, pp. 17–19.
37. George Arney, 'Non-Violent Protest in Kashmir', *BBC World Service*, 14 October 2008; Sheikh Mushtaq, 'India to Free Protesters in Kashmir Peace Move', *Reuters*, 30 September 2010; Ashiq Hussain, 'Valley Victims Accept Compensation, Quietly', *Hindustan Times*, 20 February 2011.
38. Khalra's investigation was later continued by Sikh human rights activists. For an overview, see Ensaaf, 'The Punjab Mass Cremations Case: India Burning the Rule of Law', Freemont, 2007; and Ensaaf and Benetech HRDAG, 'Violent Deaths and Enforced Disappearances During the Counterinsurgency in

Punjab, India: A Preliminary Quantitative Analysis', Freemont and Palo Alto, 2009.

39. For a comparative analysis of counter-insurgency campaigns in Punjab and Kashmir, see Cynthia Keppley Mahmood, 'Trials by Fire: Dynamics of Terror in Punjab and Kashmir', in Jeffrey Sluka (ed.), *Death Squad: The Anthropology of State Terror*. Philadelphia, PA: University of Pennsylvania Press, 2000, pp. 70–90.

40. Minority Rights Group International, 'Adivasis', *World Directory of Minorities and Indigenous Peoples*, at: minorityrights.org (accessed March 2015).

41. 'Naxalism', in the words of Manmohan Singh (then prime minister of India), 'remains the biggest internal security challenge facing [India].' 'Naxalism Biggest Threat to Internal Security: Manmohan', *The Hindu*, 24 May 2010. For an overview of India's war against the Maoists, see also Nandini Sundar, 'At War with Oneself: Constructing Naxalism as India's Biggest Security Threat', in Michael Kugelman (ed.), *India's Contemporary Security Challenges*. Washington DC: Woodrow Wilson International Center for Scholars, 2011.

42. For a gripping account of this 'people's war', see Arundhati Roy, 'Walking with the Comrades', *Outlook*, 29 March 2010.

43. R.S.D. Dogra, *Nation Keepers: Central Reserve Police Force*. New Delhi: APH Publishing, 2004, pp. 1–9. See also C.P. Bhambri, 'Role of Paramilitary Forces in Centre-State Relations', *Economic and Political Weekly* (13: 17), 1978, pp. 735–37.

44. International Institute for Strategic Studies, 'Asia', p. 252.

45. Nandini Sundar, 'Why Everyone Speaks the Flowing Language of Blood', *Outlook*, 26 October 2009; and 'The Trophies of Operation Green Hunt: When Rape is Routine and There's a Paucity of Condemning Voices', *Outlook*, 5 July 2010.

46. Human Rights Watch, 'Between Two Sets of Guns: Attacks on Civil Society Activists in India's Maoist Conflict', New York, 2012.

47. Shashank Bengali, 'India Cracks Down on Greenpeace, Other Environmental Groups', *Los Angeles Times*, 13 January 2015.

48. This description of Salwa Judum and Special Police Officers (SPO) is primarily based on three sources: Human Rights Watch, 'Being Neutral is Our Biggest Crime: Government, Vigilante and Naxalite Abuses in India's Chhattisgarh State', New York, 2008, pp. 29–45; People's Union for Democratic Rights, 'Where the State Makes War on its Own People: A Report on Violation of People's Rights During the Salwa Judum Campaign', New Delhi, 2006; Scott Gates and Kaushik Roy, *Unconventional Warfare in South Asia: Shadow Warriors and Counterinsurgency*. Farnham: Ashgate, 2014, p. 81.

49. Tekendra Parmar, 'Drones in India', Center for the Study of the Drone, at: dronecenter.bard.edu (accessed March 2015).

50. Harriet Sherwood, 'Israel is World's Largest Drone Exporter', *The Guardian*, 20 May 2013; and Udi Etsion, 'India to Spend $1b on Israeli Weapons', *Ynetnews*, 18 February 2015.

51. These are approximated figures, which I calculated using the SIPRI database, at: armstrade.sipri.org (accessed March 2015).

52. For an overview of Israel's drone exports, see Drone Wars UK, 'Israel and the Drone Wars: Examining Israel's Production, Use and Proliferation of UAVs', Oxford, 2014.

53. Figures (budget and troop numbers) cited in this paragraph are based on estimates by the International Institute for Strategic Studies. To calculate India's military expenditure, I have also relied on datasets available via the World Bank, at: data.worldbank.org

54. For an account of the first encounter killing in Mumbai, see 'Who was Manya Surve?', *Afternoon Despatch and Courier*, 8 June 2012.

55. My description of Ibrahim and the Indian Mafia is primarily based on two sources: S. Hussain Zaidi, *Dongri to Dubai: Six Decades of Mumbai Mafia*. New Delhi: Roli Books, 2012; and Suketu Mehta, *Maximum City: Bombay Lost and Found*. New York, Vintage, 2004, pp. 133–35. That Ibrahim is now based in Pakistan is a claim advanced by Indian intelligence agencies, see, for example, Divyesh Nair, 'Dawood Ibrahim Still Enjoying Patronage of Pakistan's ISI?' *Daily News & Analysis*, 6 May 2015.

4. Nepal: The Royal Army

1. In this chapter, my description of the Doramba massacre is based on three sources: National Human Rights Commission, 'Doramba Incident, Ramechhap: On-the-Spot Inspection and Report of the Investigation Committee', Kathmandu, 2003; Kanak Mani Dixit, 'Remembering Doramba', *The Kathmandu Post*, 16 August 2012; and Susan Appleyard, 'Forensic Archaeology in Nepal', in Mike W.J. Groen, *et al.* (eds), *Forensic Archaeology: A Global Perspective*, Oxford: Wiley Blackwell, 2015, pp. 309–17.

2. For a discussion on the role of martyrdom in the people's war, see Marie Lecomte Tilouine, 'Martyrs and Living Martyrs of the People's War in Nepal', *Samaj* (4), 2010.

3. Human Rights Watch, 'Between a Rock and a Hard Place: Civilians Struggle to Survive in Nepal's Civil War', New York, 2004, pp. 53–63.

4. For an overview, see T. Louise Brown, *The Challenge to Democracy in Nepal: A Political History*, London: Routledge, 1996.

5. For more on the CPN-M's relationship with CCOMPOSA, see Bishnu Raj Upreti, 'External Links of the Maoist Insurgency in Nepal', in Jaideep Saikia and Ekaterina Stepanova (eds), *Terrorism: Patterns of Internationalization*, New Delhi: Sage, 2009, pp. 102–03.

6. Daniel Lak, 'Nepal's Shining Path', *Nepali Times*, 5–11 June 2009; Alastair Lawson, 'Who are Nepal's Maoist Rebels?', *BBC*, 6 June 2005.

7. Luni Piya and Keshav Maharjan, 'Protracted People's War in Nepal: An Analysis from the Perspective of Azar's Theory of Protracted Social Conflict', *Journal of International Development and Cooperation* (15: 1–2), 2009, pp. 185–203. This paper also contains the complete list of Maoist demands and goals.

8. For a discussion regarding the politics behind deployment of the RNA and declaration of state of emergency, see Dhruba Kumar, 'The Royal Nepal Army', *Himal*, March 2006.

9. In some accounts, Nepal's war on 'Maoist terrorism' was indeed engineered (as opposed to sponsored) by the United States. See, for example, John Mage, 'The Nepali Revolution and International Relations', *Economic and Political Weekly* (42: 20), 2007, pp. 1834–1939.

10. Human Rights Watch, 'Between a Rock and a Hard Place', p. 14.

11. This demand for immunity and extraordinary powers was discussed in detail by Dhruva Kumar, in his essay published by *Himal* (see Note 8).

12. For a detailed legal analysis of TADO/TADA, see International Bar Association, 'Nepal in Crisis: Justice Caught in the Cross-Fire', pp. 37–56.

13. For an overview of Nepal's national/public security laws, see International Commission of Jurists, 'Nepal: National Security Laws and Human Rights Implications', Geneva, 2009.

14. International Commission of Jurists, 'Nepal: National Security Laws and Human Rights Implications', p. 10.

15. Many of these cases were documented by Nepalese human rights groups. For a collection of statements by torture survivors, see Advocacy Forum, 'Sharing Experiences of Torture Survivors', Kathmandu, 2006, pp. 7–28.

16. My description of the Maharajgunj torture centre is primarily based on: Office of the High Commissioner for Human Rights (OHCHR), 'Report of Investigation into Arbitrary Detention, Torture and Disappearances at Maharajgunj RNA Barracks, Kathmandu, in 2003–2004', Kathmandu, 2006.

17. OHCHR, 'Report of Investigation into Arbitrary Detention, Torture and Disappearances at Maharajgunj RNA Barracks', p. 57.

18. To describe the torture and murder of Maina Sunuwar, I have relied on three sources: OHCHR, 'The Torture and Death in Custody of Maina Sunuwar: Summary of Concerns', Kathmandu, 2006; Advocacy Forum, 'Maina Sunuwar: Separating Fact from Fiction', Kathmandu, 2010; Appleyard, 'Forensic Archaeology in Nepal', pp. 314–15.

19. Phanindra Dahal, 'As Nepali Peacekeepers' Number Falls, Army Turns to Govt for Help', *The Kathmandu Post*, 14 September 2012.

20. These figures (deployment of Nepalese peacekeepers) are based on monthly and yearly troop statistics released by the Department of Peacekeeping Operations, at: un.org/en/peacekeeping

21. For an in-depth investigation of Nepal's participation in peacekeeping missions, see Advocacy Forum, 'Vetting in Nepal: Challenges and Issues', Kathmandu, 2014.

22. Randy W. Berry, 'Nepal: UNPKO Officer Repatriated and Detained', leaked US diplomatic cable (09KATHMANDU1135), Kathmandu, 14 December 2009, available via WikiLeaks.

23. According to Human Rights Watch, 'dozens of Nepal army officers, including Maj. Basnet and another soldier charged with Maina's murder, had received training at Sandhurst military academy in the UK. See Human Rights Watch,

'UK: Insist on Accountability as Nepal Army Chief Visits', statement, London, 2010.

24. According to International Crisis Group, 'since the mid 1950s a limited number of [Nepal Army] officers received training at Sandhurst every year and many top officers have attended the academy.' See International Crisis Group, 'Nepal: Peace and Justice', Brussels, 2010, pp. 21–22.

25. Friedrich Ebert Stiftung, 'Political Developments in Nepal – 2002', Kathmandu, 2003.

26. Mark Curtis, *Unpeople: Victims of British Policy*, London: Vintage, 2004, p. 158.

27. Human Rights Watch, 'Between a Rock and a Hard Place', p. 90.

28. Ibid., pp. 89–90.

29. This secret programme was first noted by Mark Curtis, in a book published in 2003. Details about Operation Mustang, however, were revealed for the first time in 2014, in a book by the journalist Thomas Bell. See Mark Curtis, *Web of Deceit: Britain's Real Role in the World*, London: Vintage, 2003, p. 81; Thomas Bell, *Kathmandu*, Gurgaon, Haryana: Random House, 2014; Gyanu Adhikari, 'UK's Covert Acts During Nepalese Civil War', *Al Jazeera*, 19 September 2014; Agence France-Presse, 'Britain Accused of Conniving at Torture of Maoists in Nepal's Civil War', *The Guardian*, 31 August 2014.

30. Celia Dugger, 'Nepal Says over 400 Rebels are Dead after Several Battles', *New York Times*, 6 May 2002.

31. Human Rights Watch, 'Between a Rock and a Hard Place', p. 79–80.

32. Here, my description of these military aid programmes (arms transfer and training) is based on two sources: Human Rights Watch, 'Between a Rock and a Hard Place', pp. 84–89; and Congressional Research Service, 'Nepal: Background and US Relations', (RL31599), 2006, pp. 17–19.

33. A description of the IMET programme is available on the US Department of State website, at: state.gov (accessed April 2015). The programme is overseen by the Bureau of Political Military Affairs. This, of course, is one of the key tools which is used by the United States government for sponsoring state terror in South Asia and elsewhere.

34. For an analysis of the politics behind Indian sponsorship of the Nepalese regime, see Rabindra Mishra, 'India's Role in Nepal's Maoist Insurgency', *Asian Survey* (44: 5), 2004, pp. 627–46. According to Human Rights Watch,

> India has been instrumental in opposing a larger United Nations or international role in monitoring the conflict in Nepal. India's opposition to a larger UN or international role in Nepal – including opposition to international monitors and international mediation of the conflict – is fuelled mostly by India's own domestic concerns. For years, India has opposed similar attempts to introduce international rights monitors or international mediation in the conflict in Kashmir, and India's stance has been that bringing international monitors or mediation to Nepal would set a negative precedent for its own attempts to oppose such a move in Kashmir.

See Human Rights Watch, 'Between a Rock and a Hard Place', p. 92.

35. Ibid., pp. 92–93.

36. Figures (budget and troop numbers) cited in this paragraph are based on estimates/annual assessments by the International Institute for Strategic Studies (as published in *The Military Balance*). To calculate Nepal's military expenditure, I have also relied on datasets available via the World Bank, at: data.worldbank.org and IndexMundi, at: indexmundi.com

37. For an overview/summary of events, see Kanak Mani Dixit, 'The Spring of Dissent: People's Movement in Nepal', *India International Centre Quarterly* (33: 1), 2006, pp. 113–25.

38. 'Nepal Votes to Abolish Monarchy', *BBC*, 28 May 2008.

39. Human Rights Watch, 'Between a Rock and a Hard Place', p. 83.

40. For an update, see Anne Mocko and Dorji Penjore, 'Nepal and Bhutan in 2014: New Governments, Old Problems', *Asian Survey* (55: 1), 2015, pp. 75–81.

41. For a review of the campaign for truth and reconciliation, see Advocacy Forum, 'Nepal: Transitional Justice at Crossroads', Kathmandu, 2014.

5. Pakistan: Agents of the State

1. Human Rights Commission of Pakistan, 'Hopes, Fears and Alienation in Balochistan: Report of an HRCP Fact-Finding Mission', Lahore, 2012 pp. 68–71.

2. Human Rights Watch, 'We Can Torture, Kill or Keep You for Years: Enforced Disappearances by Pakistan Security Forces in Balochistan', New York, 2011, pp. 88–89; Human Rights Commission of Pakistan, 2012, p. 69; Malik Siraj Akbar, 'Pakistan vs. Balochistan', *Huffington Post*, 15 February 2012.

3. Zahid Gishkori, 'Revealing Figures: More than Half of Balochistan is Poor', *The Express Tribune*, 25 February 2013.

4. For an overview of the conflict in Balochistan, see Adeel Khan, 'Renewed Ethnonationalist Insurgency in Balochistan, Pakistan: The Militarized State and Continuing Economic Deprivation', *Asian Survey* (49: 6), 2009, pp. 1071–91.

5. As Murtaza Haider put it:

> The insurgencies in Balochistan, in Pakistan and in Jammu and Kashmir (J&K) in India have much in common. An armed struggle by the youth has taken root in both places. The 2000-plus bullet-riddled bodies recovered from the unmarked graves in four districts in Indian occupied Kashmir as well as the mutilated bodies of hundreds of Balochi youth left to rot in the desert in Balochistan are examples of how violence is destroying the social order and the moral fabric of Balochs and Kashmiris alike.

> See Murtaza Haider, 'Drawing Parallels Between Balochistan and Kashmir', *Dawn*, 4 January 2012. Also of note here is Pakistani repression in the Pakistan-occupied part of Kashmir, see Human Rights Watch, 'With Friends Like This: Human Rights Violations in Azad Kashmir', New York, 2006.

6. Human Rights Watch, 'We Can Torture, Kill or Keep You for Years', p. 11.

7. See Declan Walsh, 'Pakistan's Secret Dirty War', *The Guardian*, 29 March 2011.

8. According to Human Rights Watch:

Witnesses frequently described the perpetrators as armed men in civilian clothes, usually arriving in one or more four-door pickup trucks. The witnesses typically referred to these assailants as representatives of the 'agencies', a term commonly used to describe the intelligence agencies, including the Directorate for Inter-Services Intelligence (ISI), Military Intelligence (MI) and the Intelligence Bureau (IB).

See Human Rights Watch, 'We Can Torture, Kill or Keep You for Years', p. 3.

9. Ibid.
10. Human Rights Watch, 'Soiled Hands: The Pakistan Army's Repression of the Punjab Farmer's Movement', 2004, p. 14–15; World Sindhi Congress, 'Extra-judicial Killings of Sindhi Political Activists in 2014', Hertfordshire, 2014.
11. See Laurent Gayer, 'Guns, Slums and "Yellow Devils": A Genealogy of Urban Conflicts in Karachi, Pakistan', *Modern Asian Studies* (41: 3), 2007, pp. 515–44.
12. Imran Ayub, 'Analysis: Encounter Policy Unsustainable', *Dawn*, 20 November 2014; Jon Boone, 'Pakistan Police Take Harsh Justice to the Streets: "Mostly we get the right people"', *The Guardian*, 17 November 2014.
13. Vasundhara Sirnate, 'The Entrepreneurs of Violence', *The Hindu*, 25 December 2014.
14. Declan Walsh, 'Taliban Besiege Pakistan School, Leaving 145 Dead', *New York Times*, 16 December 2014; '132 Children Killed in Peshawar School Attack', *The Express Tribune*, 16 December 2014.
15. 'Children Massacred in Pakistan School Attack', *Al Jazeera*, 17 December 2014.
16. Jon Boone, 'Heavy Fighting at Karachi Airport as Militants and Security Forces Clash', *The Guardian*, 8 June 2014.
17. Abdul Manan, 'Zarb-e-Azb Inflicted Fatal Blow on Terrorists: PM', *The Express Tribune*, 10 December 2014.
18. 'Pakistan's IDPs Reach Record One Million', *Al Jazeera*, 1 September 2014.
19. Syed Shoaib Hasan, 'Pakistan Army Accused of Extrajudicial Killings in Swat', *BBC*, 16 July 2010.
20. Dean Nelson and Emal Khan, 'Pakistan "Army Death Squad Hangs Taliban Body from Lamp Post"', *The Telegraph*, 19 August 2009.
21. Ashfaq Yusufzai, 'Pakistan: Local Residents Tacitly Approve of Swat Killings', *Inter Press Service*, 1 October 2009.
22. See Amnesty International, '"A Bullet has been Chosen for You": Attacks on Journalists in Pakistan', London, 2014; Umar Cheema, 'Letter from Islamabad: Inside the Deadly War Against Pakistan Media', Global Investigative Journalism Network, 1 July 2014; and Phelim Kine, 'Dispatches: Censoring Pakistan's Epidemic of Violence', Human Rights Watch, 9 April 2015.
23. Omar Waraich, 'Pakistan Journalist Vanishes: Is the ISI Involved?', *Time*, 31 May 2011.
24. Jane Perlez and Eric Schmitt, 'Pakistan's Spies Tied to Slaying of a Journalist', *New York Times*, 4 July 2011.
25. 'Aid to Pakistan by the Numbers', Center for Global Development, at: cgdev.org (accessed March 2015).

26. See Gary J. Bass, *The Blood Telegram: Nixon, Kissinger and a Forgotten Genocide*, London: Hurst & Company, 2014.
27. For an early account of this relationship, see Robert Wirsing and James Roherty, 'The United States and Pakistan', *International Affairs* (58: 4), 1982, pp. 588–609.
28. 'Aid to Pakistan by the Numbers', Center for Global Development, at: cgdev. org (accessed March 2015).
29. Ibid.
30. Congressional Research Service, 'Pakistan: US Foreign Assistance', (R41856), 2013, p. 16.
31. Ibid., p. 25.
32. The facts and figures cited in this paragraph are based on the Congressional Research Service, 'Pakistan: US Foreign Assistance', pp. 17–22.
33. Pervez Musharraf, *In the Line of Fire: A Memoir*, London: Simon & Schuster, 2006, p. 237.
34. See Ian Cobain, 'The Truth about Torture: Britain's Catalogue of Shame', *The Guardian*, 8 July 2009; *Cruel Britannia: A Secret History of Torture*, London: Portobello, 2012; Human Rights Watch, 'Cruel Britannia: British Complicity in the Torture and Ill-Treatment of Terror Suspects in Pakistan', New York, 2009.
35. Human Rights Watch, 'Cruel Britannia', p. 31–32.
36. For a brief history of extraordinary rendition, see Jane Mayer, 'Outsourcing Torture: The Secret History of America's "Extraordinary Rendition" Program', *The New Yorker*, 14 February 2005.
37. Asif Ali Zardari, 'Sino-Pakistan Relations Higher than Himalayas', *China Daily*, 23 February 2009.
38. See official records of Security Council meetings: 1606 (4 December 1971), 1607 (5 December 1971) and 1613 (13 December 1971).
39. The US delegation, incidentally, was led by George H. W. Bush, who was then serving as the US ambassador to the United Nations.
40. My description of China–Pakistan relationship is primarily based on two sources: Lisa Curtis, 'China's Military and Security Relationship with Pakistan', The Heritage Foundation, 26 May 2009; and David Scott, 'South Asia in China's Strategic Calculus', in Shaun Breslin (ed.), *Handbook of China's International Relations*, London: Routledge, 2010, pp. 210–11.

   For an early account of Pakistani arms export and production licence arrangements with China and other countries, see CIA Directorate of Intelligence, 'Pakistan: Defense Industry Struggles for Self-Sufficiency: A Research Paper' [DOC_0000107402], 1989, available via CIA FOIA reading room, at: foia.cia.gov
41. Human Rights Watch, 'We Can Torture, Kill or Keep You for Years', p. 22. For an overview of the ATA, see also Amnesty International, 'Pakistan: Legalizing the Impermissible: The New Anti-Terrorism Law', London, 1997.
42. For an overview of the PPA, see International Commission of Jurists, 'Protection of Pakistan Bill, 2014: An Affront to Human Rights', Geneva, 2014.

43. International Institute for Strategic Studies, 'Asia', *The Military Balance* (115: 1), 2015, p. 276. GDP and government expenditure percentages are according to the datasets available via the World Bank, at: data.worldbank.org
44. International Institute for Strategic Studies, 'Asia', p. 276.
45. According to International Institute for Strategic Studies:

    Pakistan's nuclear and conventional forces have traditionally been orientated and structured against a prospective threat from India. Since 2008, however, a priority for the army has been counter-insurgency operations, mainly against Islamist groups for which forces have been redeployed from the Indian border.

    As noted by the Congressional Research Service (see Note 30), this exact change or reorientation was demanded by the United States Department of Defense.
46. International Institute for Strategic Studies, 'Asia', pp. 276–78.
47. Ibid., p. 279.
48. Ibid., p. 279.
49. Hassan Abbas, 'Transforming Pakistan's Frontier Corps', *Terrorism Monitor/ Jamestown Foundation* (5: 6), 2007.
50. 'Pakistan Rangers (Sindh)', Pakistan Army, at: pakistanarmy.gov.pk (accessed March 2015).
51. Bruce Loudon, 'Pakistan Clips Spy Agency's Wings', *The Australian*, 28 July 2008.
52. For a brief history of the ISI, see Sean P. Winchell, 'Pakistan's ISI: The Invisible Government', *International Journal of Intelligence and Counterintelligence* (16), 2003, pp. 374–88.
53. In describing the Pakistani National Security Council, I have relied on two sources: Pakistan Institute of Legislative Development and Transparency, 'National Security Council: A Debate on Institutions and Processes for Decision-Making on Security Issues', Islamabad, 2012 [2005]; and Ayesha Siddiqa, *Military Inc.: Inside Pakistan's Military Economy*, London: Pluto Press, 2007. See also 'DCC to be Reconstituted as Committee on National Security', *Dawn*, 22 August 2013.
54. For an in-depth analysis of Milbus, see Siddiqa, *Military Inc.: Inside Pakistan's Military Economy*.
55. Ibid., p. 18.
56. Ibid., p. 5.

6. Sri Lanka: White Vans

1. London (along with other cities across the globe) was also the site of massive anti-war demonstrations by members of the Tamil diaspora.
2. My description of this event (including the quotations) is based on two articles published online by the Sri Lankan Ministry of Defense, 'Bodhi Puja in London to Bless President and the Armed Forces', and 'President and War Heroes

Blessed by Bodhi Puja at Kingsbury Buddhist Vihara London UK', at: defence. lk (accessed March 2015).

3. For an overview of this conflict and Sri Lanka's political history, see Crispin Bates, *Subalterns and Raj: South Asia Since 1600*. London: Routledge, 2007, pp. 279–97.

4. 'Up to 100,000 Killed in Sri Lanka's Civil War: UN', *Agence France Presse* (via *ABC News*), 20 May 2009; 'Sri Lanka: Government Welcomes Refugee Repatriation from India', *IRIN*, 30 August 2012.

5. 'Sri Lanka Street Party Celebrates End of Civil War', *CNN*, 19 May 2009.

6. The text of this speech (English translation) is available via the South Asia Terrorism Portal 'President's Speech to Parliament on the Defeat of LTTE', at: satp.org (accessed March 2015).

7. For details, see 'Sri Lanka War Crimes: Main Allegations', *BBC*, 17 June 2011; International Crisis Group, 'War Crimes in Sri Lanka', Brussels, 2010, pp. 9–27.

8. Jonathan Miller, 'Sri Lanka War Crimes Soldiers Ordered to Finish the Job', *Channel 4 News*, 27 July 2011. Channel 4 (with ITN) also produced two documentary films, *Sri Lanka's Killing Fields* and *Sri Lanka's Killing Fields: War Crimes Unpunished*, that revealed evidence of Sri Lankan war crimes and crimes against humanity. These can be viewed on the Channel 4 website, at: channel4.com

9. This description of the Sri Lankan national security state is primarily based on three essays by Jayadeva Uyangoda, political scientist and commentator, see Jayadeva Uyangoda, 'Sri Lanka: The State Changes Face', *Economic and Political Weekly* (43: 43), 2008, pp. 8–9; 'Sri Lanka in 2009: From Civil War to Political Uncertainties', *Asian Survey* (50: 1), 2010, pp. 104–11; 'Sri Lanka in 2010', *Asian Survey* (51: 1), 2011, pp. 131–37.

10. For an analysis, see Tessa Bartholomeusz, *In Defense of Dharma: Just-War Ideology in Buddhist Sri Lanka*. London: Routledge, 2002. Also Richard Gombrich and Gananath Obeyesekere, *Buddhism Transformed: Religious Change in Sri Lanka*. New Delhi: Princeton University Press, 1990 [1988], pp. 384–410.

11. Valerie Fowler, 'Embassy Colombo P1 Request', leaked US diplomatic cable [09COLOMBO1069], Colombo, 25 September 2009, available via WikiLeaks.

12. 'There are No Human Rights in Sri Lanka', *Amnesty USA*, 30 April 2013.

13. For details about de Zoysa's murder, see 'BBC Drama on Richard de Zoysa', BBC Sinhala, 24 November 2008.

14. E. W. Karunadasa, 'Richard de Soysa, Manorani Saravanamuttu Commemorated', *Daily News* (Sri Lanka), 18 February 2005; Immigration and Refugee Board of Canada, 'Sri Lanka: Information on the Group Mothers' Front and How Members are Treated by the Authorities', 1995, available via Refworld.

15. Ameen Izzadeen, 'Rights, Realism and Duplicity: The Two Faces of Rajapaksa', *Al Jazeera*, 25 November 2013. According to a biographical note:

> From the start of his career, Rajapaksa adopted a centre-left political stance, identifying himself with labour rights and becoming a champion of human rights. He was a leading member of the Parliamentarians for Human Rights.

He came into prominence as a champion of human rights, together with Dr Manorani Saravanamuttu, of the Mother's Front, which organized the mothers of the 'disappeared' in the white terror of 1988–90. The Visva Bharati University of Calcutta in India conferred on him the title Professor Emeritus for his record on human rights.

See 'President's Profile', President's Fund of Sri Lanka, at: presidentsfund.gov. lk (accessed March 2015).

16. For details, see Amnesty International, 'Sri Lanka's Assault on Dissent', London, 2013; and James Crabtree, 'Censorship and Threat of Violence Hang over Sri Lanka's Press', *Financial Times*, 8 November 2013.

17. Prageeth Missing Due to Chemical Weapon Probe', *BBC Sinhala*, 28 January 2011.

18. Human Rights Watch, 'Recurring Nightmare: State Responsibility for Disappearances and Abductions in Sri Lanka', New York, 2008, pp. 136–207.

19. Human Rights Watch, 'Recurring Nightmare', pp. 3–4.

20. I have calculated these figures (number of disappearances) based on annual reports and statistics published by the WGEID, these are available from the OHCHR website, at: ohchr.org

21. See 'Commissions of Inquiry: Sri Lanka', United States Institute of Peace, at: usip.org (accessed March 2015).

22. Human Rights Watch, 'Recurring Nightmare', p. 16.

23. Ibid.

24. Ibid., p. 19.

25. I have calculated this total amount based on annual military spending data available via IndexMundi, at: indexmundi.com and the World Bank, at: data. worldbank.org

26. These numbers are based on annual military expenditure data available via the World Bank, at: data.worldbank.org

27. This colonial law indeed was the mother of all black laws in Sri Lanka. See Abizer Zanzi, 'Sri Lanka's Emergency Laws', *Seminar* (512), 2002; International Commission of Jurists, 'Sri Lanka: Emergency Laws and International Standards', Geneva, 2009, pp. ii, 12.

28. International Commission of Jurists, 'Sri Lanka: Emergency Laws and International Standards', pp. 18–19.

29. Human Rights Watch, 'Recurring Nightmare', pp. 34–37.

30. Ibid., p. 38.

31. 'Tamil Tigers: Suicide Bombing Innovators', *NPR*, 21 May 2009; Preeti Bhattacharji, 'Backgrounder: Liberation Tigers of Tamil Eelam', Council on Foreign Relations, 20 May 2009.

32. The politics behind international arms transfer to Sri Lanka was discussed in detail in a review published by the Swedish Peace and Arbitration Society. See Siemon Wezeman, 'Fuelling the Sri Lankan Conflict: Arms Transfers to Sri Lanka', in Jonas Lindberg, *et al.* (eds), *Arms Trade with Sri Lanka – Global Business, Local Costs*. Stockholm: Pax förlag, 2011, pp. 40–51.

33. This description (of Chinese arms transfer to Sri Lanka) is primarily based on two sources: Wezeman, 'Fuelling the Sri Lankan Conflict', pp. 45–46; and Saferworld, 'China and Conflict-Affected States: Between Principle and Pragmatism', London, 2012, pp. 25–60.
34. Saferworld, 'China and Conflict-Affected States', p. 42.
35. Hannah Gardner, 'China's Aid Revealed in Sri Lanka's Victory Parade', *The National* (UAE), 9 June 2009.
36. Saferworld, 'China and Conflict-Affected States', p. 46.
37. Ibid.
38. Ibid.
39. Ibid.
40. Ibid.
41. Ibid.
42. Dinouk Colombage, 'Sri Lanka's Surging Cash Reliance on China', *Al Jazeera*, 26 August 2014.
43. In describing Israeli sponsorship of Sri Lanka's national security machinery, I relied on two sources: Benjamin Beit-Hallahmi, *The Israeli Connection: Whom Israel Arms and Why*. London: IB Tauris, 1987, pp. 33–36; and P.A. Ghosh, *Ethnic Conflict in Sri Lanka and Role of Indian Peace Keeping Force (IPKF)*. New Delhi: APH Publishing, 1999, pp. 55–58.
44. This description (of Israeli arms transfer to Sri Lanka) is primarily based on: Wezeman, 'Fuelling the Sri Lankan Conflict', pp. 48-49. See also Drone Wars UK, 'Israel and the Drone Wars: Examining Israel's Production, Use and Proliferation of UAVs', Oxford, 2014, pp. 20, 23; and Krisna Saravanamuttu, 'Israel Advises Sri Lanka on Slow-Motion Genocide', *Electronic Intifada*, 30 July 2013.
45. Wezeman, 'Fuelling the Sri Lankan Conflict', pp. 46–47.
46. Tisaranee Gunasekara, 'A Garrison State?', *Himal*, 13 October 2014; Darini Rajasingham-Senanayake, 'Is Post-War Sri Lanka Following the Military Business Model?', *Economic and Political Weekly* (46: 14), 2011, pp. 27–30.

7. State Terror in Post-Colonial South Asia

1. For a general overview of the history of colonial and post-colonial South Asia, see Crispin Bates, Subalterns and Raj: South Asia Since 1600, London: Routledge, 2007.
2. Or, a 'British protectorate', see James Onley, 'The Raj Reconsidered: British India's Informal Empire and Spheres of Influence in Asia and Africa', *Asian Affairs* (40:1), 2009, pp. 44–62.
3. A fascinating account of the British relationship with the rulers of Nepal and the recruitment of Gurkha soldiers was given by Brigadier General C.G. Bruce in 1925, see C.G. Bruce, and W. Brook Northey, 'Nepal', *The Geographical Journal* (65: 4), 1925, pp. 281–98.
4. As Chris Bellamy argues, Gurkha soldiers were most often deployed by British generals and military strategists as 'special forces', especially in emergency situations. In other words, they were the early examples of what we now know

as 'special operations forces' – deployed by the national security state, in times of crisis. For an overview, see Chris Bellamy, *The Gurkhas: Special Force*. London: John Murray, 2011.

5. Kathleen Ho, 'Structural Violence as a Human Rights Violation', *Essex Human Rights Review* (4: 2), 2007.

6. Indeed, ruling without consent or coercive governance and structural violence (in the form of deprivation) are the main causes of major ethnic conflicts (insurgencies) in South Asia. See P. Sahadevan, 'Ethnic Conflicts and Militarism in South Asia', *International Studies* (39: 2), 2002, pp. 103–38.

7. As I briefly note in Chapter 8, prioritising the state's capacity for violence (tied to militarism) over its capacity for delivering public goods (tied to human development) is a feature of the national security state.

8. According to Seema Kazi:

> The use of terror, torture, rape, sexual abuse, extrajudicial killing and enforced disappearance by armed forces is not viewed as unconscionable, or understood as the flagrant breach of law and legality that it is. On the contrary, protecting the armed forces engaging in such practices is considered essential towards the maintenance of law and order and, by extension, to the survival of the nation itself. As state repression is legitimised as law-making violence, local resistance against the status quo is discredited and de-legitimised as law-breaking opposition and met with all the coercive power at the disposal of the national government.

See Seema Kazi, 'States of Denial', *Himal*, 31 October 2014.

9. For a discussion, see Udayon Misra, 'The Margins Strike Back: Echoes of Sovereignty and the Indian State', *India International Centre Quarterly* (32: 2/3), 2005, pp. 265–74.

10. Arundhati Roy, 'Capitalism: A Ghost Story', *Outlook*, 26 March 2012.

11. For details about these cases, see Malavika Vyawahare, 'A Conversation with Human Rights Activist Binayak Sen', *India Ink* (*New York Times*), 10 December 2012; Arundhati Roy, 'Professor, POW', *Outlook*, 18 May 2015.

12. Sanjib Baruah and Rajesh Ahuja, 'Narendra Modi Govt Cracks Down on NGOs, Prepares Hitlist', *Hindustan Times*, 24 January 2015.

13. For an analysis, see B.K. Roy, 'On the Questions of Migration in India: Challenges and Opportunities', *GeoJournal* (23: 3), 1991, pp. 257–68. As the author of this paper puts it: 'Rural poverty and urban misery are the two faces of the same coin which are faced by the migrants in India.'

14. This is the case in other South Asian metropolises as well. I have noted two other examples in earlier chapters: Dhaka (in Chapter 2, especially the case of Picchi Hannan) and Karachi (in Chapter 5, especially the situation in the city's slum districts). As I noted in Chapter 1, I am guided here by Frantz Fanon's discussion of the lumpenproletariat.

15. For an in-depth analysis of India's black laws and their colonial roots, see Anil Kalhan, *et al.*, 'Colonial Continuities: Human Rights, Terrorism and Security Laws in India', *Columbia Journal of Asian Law* (20: 1), 2006, pp. 93–234.

16. As proponents of international human rights law would readily point out, such immunity laws are indeed prohibited under international law. Also illegal

or prohibited are laws or proclamations that authorise or aid campaigns of torture, enforced disappearance and extrajudicial execution. These are known as *jus cogens* prohibitions. However, as I note in Chapter 9, the international human rights system offers little or no protection to the millions of victims across the globe who fall prey to black laws enacted and death squads deployed by their own governments.

17. For a note with an Indian example (TADA of 1985) of such revisions, see A.G. Noorani, 'Terrorism and Human Rights', *Economic and Political Weekly* (25: 30), 1990, p. 1621.

18. The establishment or creation of a permanent state of exception is of course a global phenomenon. As Giorgio Agamben argues:

> Modern totalitarianism can be defined as the establishment, by means of the state of exception, of a legal civil war that allows for the physical elimination not only of political adversaries but of entire categories of citizens who for some reason cannot be integrated into the political system. Since then, the voluntary creation of a permanent state of emergency (though perhaps not declared in the technical sense) has become one of the essential practices of contemporary states, including so-called democratic ones.

See Giorgio Agamben, *State of Exception*. Chicago, IL: University of Chicago Press, 2005, p. 2.

19. Talukder Maniruzzaman, 'Bangladesh: An Unfinished Revolution?', *The Journal of Asian Studies* (34: 4), 1975, pp. 891–911; Badruddin Umar, 'Martial Law Wears a New Garb', *Economic and Political Weekly* (21: 44/45), 1986, pp. 1933–34; 'End of Democratic Facade', *Economic and Political Weekly* (17: 13), 1982, p. 467; Syed Serajul Islam, 'Bangladesh in 1987: A Spectrum of Uncertainties', *Asian Survey* (28: 2), 1988, pp. 163–71; and Farid Bakht, 'Army Entrenches Itself in Bangladesh', *Economic and Political Weekly* (42: 29), 2007, pp. 2991–92.

20. Venkat Iyer, *States of Emergency: The Indian Experience*, New Delhi: Butterworths, 2000; Emma Tarlo, *Unsettling Memories: Narratives of the Emergency in Delhi*. Berkeley, CA: University of California Press, 2003.

21. 'Nepal Profile – Timeline', *BBC*, 28 April 2015; 'Nepal in State of Emergency', *The Telegraph*, 26 November 2001; 'Nepal's King Declares Emergency', *BBC*, 1 February 2005.

22. For an annotated timeline, see James Wynbrandt, *A Brief History of Pakistan*. New York: Facts on File, 2009, pp. 296–97.

23. Wynbrandt, *A Brief History of Pakistan*, pp. 297–99.

24. Iqbal Athas, 'Sri Lanka State of Emergency to End September 14', *CNN*, 25 August 2011.

25. Khalid Bin Sayeed, 'Collapse of Parliamentary Democracy in Pakistan', *Middle East Journal*, (13: 4), 1959, pp. 389–406.

26. As Robert LaPorte puts it: 'Ayub formalized the "Garrison State" nature of the Pakistani system. He made manifest what had already been implicit during the 1950s – the dominant role of the military and the civilian bureaucracy in Pakistan.' For an overview of Ayub Khan's politics, see Robert LaPorte,

'Succession in Pakistan: Continuity and Change in a Garrison State', *Asian Survey* (9: 11), 1969, pp. 842–61.

27. For an overview of the conflict in Balochistan, see Adeel Khan, 'Renewed Ethnonationalist Insurgency in Balochistan, Pakistan: The Militarized State and Continuing Economic Deprivation', *Asian Survey* (49: 6), 2009, pp. 1071–91.

28. According to a backgrounder published by the Federation of American Scientists:

> The ISI has been deeply involved in domestic politics, and has kept track of the incumbent regime's opponents. Prior to the imposition of Martial Law in 1958, ISI reported to the Commander-in-Chief of the Army (C-in-C). When martial Law was promulgated in 1958 all the intelligence agencies fell under the direct control of the President and Chief Martial Law Administrator, and the three intelligence agencies began competing to demonstrate their loyalty to Ayub Khan and his government. The ISI became even more deeply involved in domestic politics under General Yahya Khan, notably in East Pakistan, where operations were mounted to ensure that no political party should get an overall majority in the general election. An amount of Rs 29 lak was expended for this purpose, and attempts were made to infiltrate the inner circles of the Awami League. The operation was a complete disaster.

See John Pike, 'Directorate for Inter-Services Intelligence [ISI]', Federation of American Scientists, at: fas.org; a mirrored copy is available via Internet Archive Wayback Machine, at: archive.org (accessed March 2015).

29. Lawrence Ziring, 'Militarism in Pakistan: The Yahya Khan Interregnum', *Asian Affairs* (1: 6), 1974, pp. 402–20.

30. Anwar H. Syed, 'Pakistan in 1977: The Prince is Under the Law', *Asian Survey* (18: 2), 1978, pp. 117–25.

31. 'How the 1999 Pakistan Coup Unfolded', *BBC*, 23 August 2007.

32. David Rohde, 'Musharraf Declares State of Emergency', *New York Times*, 3 November 2007.

33. For an overview of these wars, see Haris Gazdar, '"Counter-Insurgencies" in Pakistan', *Economic and Political Weekly* (41: 20), 2006, pp. 1952–53.

34. For an account, see Anthony Mascarenhas, *Bangladesh: A Legacy of Blood*. London: Hodder and Stoughton, 1986, pp. 43–59.

35. For a description of this legal innovation, see Agamben, *State of Exception*, pp. 18–19.

36. Kalhan, *et al.* discuss these laws (emergency laws and martial law regimes of the British Raj) in detail, see Kalhan, *et al.*, 'Colonial Continuities', pp. 126–31.

37. See Imtiaz Omar, *Emergency Powers and the Courts in India and Pakistan*. The Hague: Kluwer Law International, 2002; and *Rights, Emergencies and Judicial Review*. The Hague: Kluwer Law International, 1996.

8. Specialists on Violence

1. See, for example, Arundhati Roy, *Broken Republic: Three Essays*. London: Hamish Hamilton, 2011, pp. ix–xii.

2. For an analysis of the politics and history of the Republic Day parade, see Srirupa Roy, *Beyond Belief: India and the Politics of Postcolonial Nationalism*. Durham, NC: Duke University Press, 2007, pp. 66–104.

3. According to a recent ranking, India has the fourth most powerful military in the world. See Amanda Macias, *et al.*, 'The 35 Most Powerful Militaries in the World', *Business Insider*, 10 July 2014.

4. According to Ranjana Sengupta:

    > India Gate, known in pre-independence New Delhi as the All India War Memorial Arch, was designed by [Edwin] Lutyens and commemorated the names of soldiers who died in the First World War. The symbolism of the Arch has always been appreciated: the Viceroy, Lord Chelmsford, felt that it expressed 'the ideal and fact of British rule over India'. Today, India Gate remains the focus of patriotic ceremonies centred on the eternal flame and the Unknown Soldier, both symbols borrowed from elsewhere, but which serve the purpose of elevating the notion of the State into a mystic realm and thereby legitimizing its demands of sacrifice and duty from common citizens.

    See Ranjana Sengupta, 'Enshrining an Imperial Tradition', *India International Centre Quarterly* (33: 2), 2006, pp. 13–26.

5. 'Republic Day: PM Modi Pays Tribute to Soldiers at Amar Jyoti Jawan', *First Post*, 26 January 2015.

6. Shelly Walia, 'Coming Soon: A "Made in USA" Republic Day Parade in India', *Quartz*, 25 January 2015; Stefano Pozzebon, 'India Put on a Spectacular Show for President Obama on Republic Day', *Business Insider*, 27 January 2015.

7. 'Armed Forces Day Today', *BSS* (via *The Daily Star*), 21 November 2010; Emily Wax, 'Sri Lankan Leader Says Tamil Rebels Nearly Defeated', *The Washington Post*, 5 February 2009; 'Pakistan Day Parade: Reviving the Lost Spirit', *Dawn*, 23 March 2015.

8. For an overview, see Kaushik Roy, *Military Manpower, Armies and Warfare in South Asia*. London: Pickering & Chatto, 2014, pp. 121–32.

9. Rajkumar (*nom de guerre*: Azad) was responding to an article by the journalist B.G. Verghese. See Azad, *Maoists in India: Writings and Interviews*. Hyderabad: Friends of Azad, 2010, pp. 132–33.

10. To this list, I must add the South Asian film industry, especially Bollywood. The brave (and forever romantic) soldier, who fights the diabolical terrorist or the deviant criminal, is a recurrent character in countless films produced by Bollywood every year. As Rubina Saigol notes:

    > Even more than television, radio or the print media, films are the most potent and virulent source of inculcating hatred. [...] The stereotypes of the Muslim terrorist and the ultra-nationalist, militaristic hero are all too common in Hindi cinema. Militaristic and nationalistic preoccupations are not only evident in films that are overtly and intentionally nationalist, they also appear in the subtext of seemingly romantic films as parallel stories, as

the background against which the love story is told and the canvas on which all Indianness is basically painted.

See Rubina Saigol, 'SAARC in 2020', in Ujjwal Kumar Singh (ed.), *Human Rights and Peace: Ideas, Laws, Institutions and Movements*. New Delhi: Sage, 2011, p. 40.

11. See Jon Boone, 'Najam Sethi, the TV Star Who Dared Take on Pakistan's Spy Agency', *The Guardian*, 18 July 2012; Tavleen Singh, 'The Real Enemies', *Indian Express*, 21 December 2008; and Amulya Ganguli, 'Rooting for Rebels', *Daily News & Analysis*, 11 May 2010.

12. Dexter Filkins, 'The Journalist and the Spies', *The New Yorker*, 19 September 2011; Omar Rashid, 'Activist Seema Azad, Husband Freed', *The Hindu*, 8 August 2012.

13. See Gardiner Harris, 'A Sri Lankan Journalist Eagerly Toes the Line', *New York Times*, 18 October 2013; Rasika Manobuddhi, *et al.*, 'Sri Lanka's Media, Five Years After the End of War', *Groundviews*, 13 May 2014; and Immigration and Refugee Board of Canada, 'Sri Lanka: Overview of Sri Lankan Media Sources, Including Affiliation or Association with Government or Opposition Parties (2011–2012)', 2013, available via Refworld.

14. As the journalist Trevor Grant notes, the demonisation of the LTTE was also recurrent in Western media's coverage of the war, see Trevor Grant, *Sri Lanka's Secrets: How the Rajapaksa Regime Gets Away with Murder*. Clayton: Monash University Publishing, 2013, pp. 195–96.

15. See, for example, 'Day 3 of Operation Green Hunt', *Times Now*, 19 September 2009; 'Operation Green Hunt: War without End', *NDTV*, 2 April 2010; 'Inside Operation Green Hunt', *Headlines Today*, 7 August 2012; 'Encounter between BSF and Naxalites', *Zee News*, 16 August 2014.

16. For example, in Pakistan, according to C. Christine Fair:

Because the Pakistan Army is a political force, it cares about maintaining a positive image among Pakistanis, and it has evolved numerous methods of manipulating its country's varied media to achieve this goal. In the past, pressure was exerted through the Ministry of Information, but in recent years ISI has established its own media cell tasked not only with monitoring international and domestic reporting about Pakistan but also with reaching out to and actively managing reporters. The military's Inter Services Public Relations (ISPR) works to ensure that 'right wing polemicists and preachers' who promote the army's preferred narratives are invited on talk shows to discuss Pakistan's 'national security', its foreign policy and the prevailing ideology of the state and the society.'

See C. Christine Fair, *Fighting to the End: The Pakistan Army's Way of War*. Oxford: Oxford University Press, 2014, p. 198.

17. For a description of 'natsec reporters' in India and their relationship with the national security bureaucracy, see Praveen Donthi, 'Known Unknowns: India's Compromised National Security Beat', *Caravan*, 1 December 2013. This, of course, is a global phenomenon. See, for example, Ken Silverstein, 'The

CIA's Mop-Up Man: LA Times Reporter Cleared Stories with Agency before Publication', *The Intercept*, 4 September 2014.

18. 'Institute for Conflict Management: An Introduction', *South Asia Terrorism Portal*, at satp.org (accessed March 2015).

19. See George Fletcher MacMunn, *The Martial Races of India*. New Delhi: Mittal, 1979 [1932]; and *The Armies of India*. New Delhi: Rupa, 2007 [1911]. See also Tan Tai Yong, *The Garrison State: Military, Government and Society in Colonial Punjab, 1849–1947*. New Delhi: Sage, 2005, pp. 59–63.

20. Daniel S. Markey, *No Exit from Pakistan*. New York: Cambridge University Press, 2013 p. 49.

21. For an overview, see Hassan N. Gardezi, 'Allah, Army and America in Pakistan', *Critical Asian Studies* (42: 1), 2010, pp. 145–63.

22. Seyed Vali Reza Nasr, *The Jamaat-i-Islami of Pakistan: The Vanguard of the Islamic Revolution*. Berkeley, CA: University of California Press, pp. 59, 133–34.

23. Mumtaz Ahmad, 'The Crescent and the Sword: Islam, the Military and Political Legitimacy in Pakistan, 1977–1985', *Middle East Journal*, (50: 3), 1996, pp. 372–86; Hamida Ghafour, 'Zia ul-Haq's Legacy in Pakistan Enduring and Toxic', *Toronto Star*, 26 August 2013.

24. Tim Hume, 'Fascists in Saffron Robes? The Rise of Sri Lanka's Buddhist Ultra-Nationalists', *CNN*, 18 July 2014; Dharisha Bastians, 'Radical Monk in Myanmar Pledges to Protect Global Buddhism', *New York Times*, 28 September 2014.

25. 'Royal Powers Curtailed Drastically', Friedrich Ebert Stiftung, 19 May 2006.

26. Ali Riaz, 'God Willing: The Politics and Ideology of Islamism in Bangladesh', *Comparative Studies of South Asia, Africa and the Middle East* (23: 1/2), 2003, pp. 301–20.

27. Mark Levene, 'The Chittagong Hill Tracts: A Case Study in the Political Economy of Creeping Genocide', *Third World Quarterly* (20: 2), 1999, pp. 339–69.

28. Pankaj Mishra, 'The Real Winners in Modi's India', *Bloomberg View*, 17 May 2015; 'Rise of the Chest-Thumpers', *Bloomberg View*, 18 June 2015; Debobrat Ghose, 'Seeking the Invincible Hindu: World Hindu Congress Wants More Defenders of the Faith', *First Post*, 22 November 2014.

29. Here, it must be noted that Kashmiri pandits indeed have been subjected to brutal attacks by violent Muslim mobs, which resulted in their exodus from the Kashmir valley. See Rahul Pandita, *Our Moon has Blood Clots: The Exodus of Kashmiri Pandits*. Noida: Random House, 2013.

30. For a discussion, see Jean Dreze, 'Militarism, Development and Democracy', *Economic and Political Weekly* (35: 14), 2000, pp. 1171–83.

31. International Institute for Strategic Studies, 'Asia', *The Military Balance* (115: 1), 2015, p. 232.

32. Ibid., pp. 232–33.

33. Kamal Ahmed, 'Bangladesh Army's Advancing Business Interests', *BBC*, 15 August 2010.

34. Jérémie Codron, 'Putting Factions Back in the Civil–Military Relations Equation: Genesis, Maturation and Distortion of the Bangladeshi Army',

free-standing article, *Samaj*, 2007; Bidanda M. Chengappa, 'Pakistan: Military Role in Civil Administration', *Strategic Analysis* (23:2), 1999, pp. 299–312; International Crisis Group, 'Reforming Pakistan's Civil Service', Brussels, 2010, pp. 2–10; Mandana Ismail Abeywickrema, 'The Militarisation of Sri Lanka's Diplomatic and Administrative Services', *The Sunday Leader*, 23 January 2011.

35. This is especially the case in 'disturbed areas' or new colonies, for example, the Chittagong Hill Tracts in Bangladesh and Northern Sri Lanka. See Amena Mohsin, 'Bangladesh: An Uneasy Accommodation', in Muthiah Alagappa (ed.), *Coercion and Governance: The Declining Political Role of the Military in Asia*. Stanford, CA: Stanford University Press, 2001, pp. 220–21; International Crisis Group, 'Sri Lanka's North II: Rebuilding Under the Military', Brussels, 2012, pp. 15–23. For an analytical overview, see also Ayesha Siddiqa, 'Thinking beyond Huntington', *Himal*, 8 November 2014.

9. International System of State Terror

1. For a brief history of the San Francisco conference, see 'San Francisco Conference – History of the United Nations,' United Nations, at: un.org (accessed March 2015).

2. The United Nations (a peacemaking organisation) was born out of a military alliance led by the United States. As Dan Plesch argues, the formation of this alliance ('war making United Nations') was crucial for defeating the Axis powers. See Dan Plesch, *America, Hitler and the UN: How the Allies won World War II and Forged a Peace*. London: IB Tauris, 2010.

3. Harry S. Truman, 'Address in San Francisco at the Closing Session of the United Nations Conference', 26 June 1945, The American Presidency Project, at: www.presidency.ucsb.edu (accessed March 2015).

4. For an account, see John Hersey, 'Hiroshima', *The New Yorker*, 31 August 1946.

5. Harry S. Truman, 'Radio Report to the American People on the Potsdam Conference', 9 August 1945, Truman Library, at: trumanlibrary.org (accessed March 2015).

6. For a critical review of this arrangement, with a focus on the United States' invasion of Iraq, see Laura J. Shepherd, '"To Save Succeeding Generations from the Scourge of War": The US, UN and the Violence of Security', *Review of International Studies* (34: 2), 2008, pp. 293–311.

7. For a historical overview of the international human rights system, see Thomas Buergenthal, 'The Evolving International Human Rights System', *The American Journal of International Law* (100: 4), 2006, pp. 783–807.

8. For a general introduction to the concept of human rights and international protection of these rights, see Andrew Clapham, *Human Rights: A Very Short Introduction*. Oxford: Oxford University Press, 2007.

9. For a discussion on the Genocide Convention of 1948, see Steven R. Ratner, *et al.*, 'The Genocide Convention after Fifty Years', Proceedings of the annual meeting of the American Society of International Law (92), 1998, pp. 1–19.

10. This, in my view, is partly facilitated by the United Nations Charter. Article 2.4 of the charter, in essence, is a prohibition on war between states (international armed conflicts). Such prohibitions, however, do not apply in the case of non-international or internal armed conflicts – an arrangement that is made explicit by Article 2.7. Dirty wars or civil wars, in other words, would fall under the 'domestic jurisdiction' of states, unless there is a decision by the Security Council (dominated by the political sponsors of those states) to intervene. This is the reason behind Chinese diplomats invoking the question of domestic jurisdiction as they discuss the Pakistani offensive in East Pakistan or the Sri Lankan offensive in northern Sri Lanka.

11. For reviews and analyses of these dirty wars, see Jeffrey Sluka (ed.), *Death Squad: The Anthropology of State Terror*. Philadelphia, PA: University of Pennsylvania Press, 2000; and Bruce B. Campbell and Arthur D. Brenner (eds), *Death Squads in Global Perspective: Murder with Deniability*. Basingstoke: Palgrave Macmillan, 2003.

12. For readers who would like to explore this further, I recommend two essays: Adriaan Bos, 'Crimes of State: In Need of Legal Rules?' in Gerard Kreijen, *et al.* (eds), *State, Sovereignty, and International Governance*. Oxford: Oxford University Press, 2002, pp. 221–38; and André Nollkaemper, 'Concurrence between Individual Responsibility and State Responsibility in International Law', *International and Comparative Law Quarterly* (52: 3), 2003, pp. 615–40.

13. Gareth Evans and Mohamed Sahnoun, 'The Responsibility to Protect', *Foreign Affairs* (81: 6), 2002, pp. 99–110.

14. Noel Dorr, 'The Responsibility to Protect: An Emerging Norm?', *Irish Studies in International Affairs* (19), 2008, pp. 189–207; David Chandler, 'Unravelling the Paradox of "The Responsibility to Protect"', *Irish Studies in International Affairs* (20), 2009, pp. 27–39.

15. As an example, see Darius Rejali's seminal study on how different methods and regimens of torture that were first developed by the core states are now being used by Third World national security states: Darius Rejali, *Torture and Democracy*. Princeton, NJ: Princeton University Press, 2009.

16. As noted in Chapter 1, Jeffrey Sluka explored this briefly in his discussion of state terror. See Sluka, *Death Squad: The Anthropology of State Terror*, pp. 7–10.

17. This order, in the words of Thomas Pogge:

> relies on latent violence in two ways. On the one hand, its stability – like that of any other realistically conceivable economic order – depends on the presence of substantial police forces that prevent and deter rule violations. On the other hand, the design of the global economic order – in contrast to that of a democratically governed state – is determined by a tiny minority of its participants whose oligarchic control of the rules ultimately also rests on a huge preponderance of military power.

See Thomas Pogge, *World Poverty and Human Rights*. Cambridge: Polity, 2008 [2002], p. 102. For a discussion on the relationship between the global economic order and Third World national security states, see also Martin Oppenheimer and Jane Canning, 'The National Security State: Repression within Capitalism', *Berkeley Journal of Sociology* (23), 1978–1979, pp. 3–33.

18. For an introductory text on the global security structure, see David N. Balaam and Bradford Dillman, *Introduction to International Political Economy*. Boston, MA: Longman, 2011, pp. 210–33.

19. The participation of soldiers from Third World (global south) national security states has been analysed at length by Philip Cunliffe. For readers who would like to explore this further, I highly recommend this ground-breaking study: Philip Cunliffe, *Legions of Peace: UN Peacekeepers from the Global South*. London: Hurst, 2013.

20. Three leaked US diplomatic cables shed light on the India–Bangladesh relationship (especially their counter-terrorism partnership) since Sheikh Hasina took power in 2008. These are available via WikiLeaks: James F. Moriarty, 'Prime Minister's Advisor Sees Hope for Breakthrough in Indo-Bangladesh Relations; Seeks USG Support', [09DHAKA1004], Dhaka, 28 October 2009; 'Bangladesh's Prime Minister Prepares for "Transformational" Visit to India', [10DHAKA27], Dhaka, 10 January 2010; and 'Government Trumpets Achievements of Prime Minister's India Visit While Opposition Claims Sellout', [10DHAKA61], Dhaka, 19 January 2010.

21. See Immigration and Refugee Board of Canada, 'Sri Lanka: Allegations of Abuses Committed by the IPKF in Sri Lanka Since July 1987', 1989, available via Refworld; and Human Rights Watch, 'Recurring Nightmare: State Responsibility for "Disappearances" and Abductions in Sri Lanka', New York, 2008, pp. 18–19.

22. This is according to statistics published by the United Nations Department of Peacekeeping Operations, at: un.org/en/peacekeeping (accessed March 2015).

23. Colum Lynch, 'India Threatens to Pull Plug on Peacekeeping', *Foreign Policy*, 14 June 2011.

24. Rahul Singh, 'UN Report says Indian Peacekeepers Face Sexual Abuse Charges', *Hindustan Times*, 24 June 2015; Bally Mutumayi, *et al.*, 'The Peacekeeper's Child', *Outlook*, 8 August 2011.

25. In its bid for Security Council membership, India has the backing of the United States. As Colum Lynch notes:

India's international identity has long been shaped by its role in U.N. peacekeeping, with more than 100,000 Indian troops having served in U.N. missions during the past 50 years. Today, India has over 8,500 peacekeepers in the field, more than twice as many as the U.N.'s five big powers combined. In supporting India's bid for a permanent seat on an enlarged Security Council last November, President Barack Obama cited 'India's long history as a leading contributor to United Nations peacekeeping mission.'

See Lynch, 'India Threatens to Pull Plug on Peacekeeping'.

26. Indrani Bagchi, 'China Emerges as Principal Opposition to UNSC Reforms', *Times of India*, 1 August 2015; Vinay Kaura, 'China on India's UNSC Bid: Neither Yes Nor No', *The Diplomat*, 3 June 2015.

27. 'Is China–Pakistan "Silk Road" a Game-Changer?', *BBC*, 22 April 2015.

28. Hannah Gardner, 'China's Aid Revealed in Sri Lanka's Victory Parade', *The National* (UAE), 9 June 2009.

29. Congressional Research Service, 'Bangladesh: Political and Strategic Developments and U.S. Interests', [R41194], 2010, p. 12.
30. These are actual and estimated figures, based on a budget justification document published by the Department of State in 2011. See Congressional Research Service, 'Bangladesh: Political and Strategic Developments and U.S. Interests', p. 13.
31. For details, see Patricia Butenis, 'Improving Bangladeshi Counter Terrorism Capabilities', [06DHAKA3453], Dhaka, 13 June 2006; and James F. Moriarty, 'Indian High Commissioner Expects Closer Counterterrorism Cooperation with New Bangladesh Government', [09DHAKA57], Dhaka, 14 January 2009, cables available via WikiLeaks.
32. James F. Moriarty, 'Engaging Bangladesh's Rapid Action Battalion: Visit by USG Interagency Assessment Team', [08DHAKA856], Dhaka, 11 August 2008, available via WikiLeaks.
33. James F. Moriarty, 'Finding Common Ground on Counterrorism Working with the UK', [09DHAKA482], Dhaka, 14 May 2009, available via WikiLeaks.
34. Fariha Karim and Ian Cobain, 'WikiLeaks Cables: Bangladeshi "Death Squad" Trained by UK Government', *The Guardian*, 21 December 2010.
35. Ian Cobain and Fariha Karim, 'Bangladesh Interrogation Centre Where Britons Were Taken to be Tortured', *The Guardian*, 17 January 2011.
36. Figures cited in this paragraph are based on monthly statistics published by the United Nations Department of Peacekeeping Operations, at: un.org/en/peacekeeping (accessed August 2015).

10. A Note from the Torture Chamber

1. 'Restricted rights', *The Daily Star*, 12 January 2007.
2. 'The Coup that Dare Not Speak its Name', *The Economist*, 18 January 2007.
3. 'Supply-side peacekeeping', *The Economist*, 21 February 2007.
4. Patricia A. Butenis, 'Ambassador and British High Commissioner Meet with Sheikh Hasina Regarding Military Coup' [07DHAKA32], Dhaka, 8 January 2007; and 'Ambassador and British High Commissioner Meet Khaleda Zia Regarding Military Coup' [07DHAKA39], Dhaka, 9 January 2007, leaked US diplomatic cables available via WikiLeaks.
5. Peter Lloyd, 'Evidence Mounts of Bangladesh Mass Torture', *Australian Broadcasting Corporation*, 8 June 2007.
6. After my release from custody (which was due to massive international pressure), I went into hiding along with my family. Eventually, we were given a safe passage out of the country. In June 2007, we arrived in Sweden and applied for political asylum, which was swiftly granted by the Swedish Migration Board. See, for details about my torture: Human Rights Watch, 'The Torture of Tasneem Khalil: How the Bangladesh Military Abuses its Power under the State of Emergency', New York, 2008; Tasneem Khalil, 'Surviving Torture in Bangladesh', *International Herald Tribune/New York Times*, 2 March 2008.

INDEX